Family, Funnies, and Other F Words

A humorous approach to self-help

ERIKA BELL

Copyright © 2021 Erika Bell

All rights reserved.

ISBN PAPERBACK: 978-1-7369954-0-2
ISBN EBOOK: 978-1-7369954-1-9

Edited by Bob Howard

DEDICATION

For my entire extended family...I love you all.

CONTENTS

	Introduction	i
1	Gold-Toothed Grandma	1
2	Hysterical Hubs	12
3	Oxymoronic Bro	34
4	Wild Card Brother	48
5	Knucklehead Uncle	62
6	Cousin Full of Contradictions	74
7	Gracious Granny	83
8	Unconventional Dad	92
9	More-Than-Meets-the-Eye Mom	112
10	Entertaining Tot	133
	Final Thoughts	159
	Acknowledgments	160
	About the Author	161

INTRODUCTION

Does the world need another self-help book? I'm not sure. But what I am sure about is that we need more laughter. More humor. More fun. And if reading any part of this book brings you any or all of those, I will be satisfied, happy, and feel a sense of accomplishment for this writing endeavor I've embarked on. And if by reading it you benefit from any of the lessons I've learned or gain anything from the self-help tidbits, then hey, that's awesome too.

The following chapters cover various family members of mine who have made a strong impact in my life in one way or another. They are characters and they are funny without trying to be. And these folks are too good not to want to share with as many people as I possibly can.

One note about the 'lessons learned' portion after each chapter. These can be lessons learned because of or in spite of. Reading each chapter, you'll know which is which.

My family is full of some of the most eclectic people. They're hard to pinpoint. Let me also say that cumulatively we're sort of a shit show, but I mean that in the nicest way possible. Nevertheless, with all of that, we all have little gems inside to give, worthy snippets to share, and a variety of things to say. I hope that makes us relatable or likeable or simply just characters you want to read about and enjoy doing so.

Now, come on in and meet the fam...

CHAPTER ONE
GOLD-TOOTHED GRANDMA

Oh, Grandma Pat, full name is Patricia if we want to be formal and fancy, and last name was Silewski.

Have fun with that one.

Shaking my head and smiling I wonder how I even begin to start describing the matriarch of my mother's side of the family. Picture a petite woman with short curly gray hair and gold front tooth. Yup, that really is such a good kicker for her; that gold tooth.

She was often yelling, not out of anger but because that was just her voice, merely the way she talked. And when she was on a roll (usually with a little help from a good Vodka Seven buzz) she would go on and on about whatever it was (usually some ridiculousness her children or grandchildren were doing). We'd call them Pat Rants and as hyped up as she ever got, she was hysterical.

She loved Josh Duhamel, as many of us do. But I'm not sure if she loved him for his looks, acting abilities, or simply the fact he was a good ole North Dakota boy from her neck of the woods. She also loved the *Bold and the Beautiful* soap opera and religiously watched it and unfortunately, she passed that interest down to both my mother and to myself. Insert eye roll here...that freaking show.

She loved Barbra Streisand and the song "My Favorite Things". She hated country music yet her favorite song was "Fishing in the Dark". Call me innocent but I never knew that song was not actually about fishing in the dark. It's about doing other things in the dark, if you catch my drift.

I wonder if she knew this too or she just liked the song as I have for so many years. Naughty grandma if she did know and shared to everyone it was a favorite of hers.

She loved being outside, but she hated the wind. The temperature could be ideal outdoors and she could be at the lake cabin or visiting a Florida beach but if it was windy, she wasn't having any part of it.

Inside or outside, you'd rarely catch her with shoes on. She'd walk around her yellow and brown shag carpet or her kitchen's linoleum, both originals from the 1960s, and then go grab her mail from outside or putz around her garden or garage, all without shoes. She didn't have cute little dainty feet made for people to look at all the time. Little is about the only word from that sentence that relates to her feet. One of the things she passed onto my mother and then passed onto me. All of us with tiny size six feet.

Although her feet were small and, in my eyes, small things often are very cute, this was not the case. She had troll feet, but they weren't hairy if you're conjuring up that image. Okay, I'm making them sound worse than they were. They weren't that bad. I don't want you to think they were gross. It wasn't like that. They were oddly shaped, having a large ball of the foot. It's somewhat difficult to explain so let's just say that they weren't the feet anyone needed to constantly see without shoes but, of course, she didn't care.

She was unapologetically herself. Her home mirrored her likeness, both perfectly old with nothing to prove.

She unintentionally coined the expression we now fondly call the Silewski Scrunch Face, a gesture she has passed on noticeably to my Uncle David and his daughter Holly and now my daughter, Pfeiffer.

I will attempt to explain so you can create a visual. It's a half smile (no teeth showing) and a half squint of your eyes. It's a combination of feeling like you just stubbed your toe and you just heard something funny. I'm not sure if this is making it clear but I'm trying to give you something to envision. While the three of them have been around grandma their entire lives, both my uncle and cousin are, as you could guess, much older than my daughter, so though we could think that they possibly picked this gesture up over after years of seeing it firsthand, that wouldn't be the case with my daughter. Pfeiffer doesn't live near them and at the time she first made the expression she wasn't even a year old, leading us to believe this funny face is genetic. Oh, how we never know what we will pass on to future generations but it's always a fun, silly reminder of her.

I have an abundance of hysterical stories with her being the star but one of my favorites involves her wetting her pants.

I'll give you a little background first. When I was younger, I would summer with her up in BFE, North Dakota. I know you must be thinking that I have such a glamorous life. As you conjure up images of extravagant parties and ritzy scenes as if it were the Hamptons or Martha's Vineyard. You'd be right. Except for the extravagance. And except for the ritz. However, there were parties. They were just held off dirt roads in a barn or a field or the like.

Even without the frills, it was still the home base for some of my favorite memories.

Not far away from that home base are our family's lake cabins. While it, too, is not as an elitist of a getaway as the aforementioned hotspots, we would escape to Minnesota and have a grand ole time.

My grandparents bought the cabins in the 1980s when they were part of a lodge. Since then, they've served as one of my family's favorite places to visit.

One day we decided to take the paddleboat out for a spin.

We were on the lake for about 40 or so minutes when she decided she had to use the bathroom. There would be no holding it. There would be no option of getting back into the cabin fast enough. What other option did she have? None. She just let loose and peed. Both of us laughing hysterically (and her yelling of course) as she did. I never let her live that down, but she didn't care. She wasn't embarrassed. It just was what it was. When ya gotta go, ya gotta go.

Her last trip down to Florida tees up another one of my favorite stories.

It's an incident that we have dubbed 'the tater tot incident'. We decided to have a GNO (Girls Night Out in case you are unfamiliar with the abbreviation) and she, myself, my mom, and my mom's friend went out for dinner and a theatre show. Grandma always ate slowly, a trait that I did not inherit but strive to emulate.

Anyway, when I say slowly, I mean slowlyyyyy. Snail speed. So, while everyone in the group finished our food, grandma still had her delicious truffle oil tater tots left. Settled on the idea that she would not leave these behind and since we did not have time to drop them in the car, she wrapped them up in a napkin and placed them in her purse.

Well, the theatre that we went to is historic and has been recently renovated. Those that run the theatre pride themselves on the appearance of the place and its upkeep and, as with many theatres, do not let you bring outside food or drinks. So yep, you guessed it, as soon as she presented her ticket the security guard investigated her purse and caught her red-handed, or rather, greasy handed. She didn't even bother to hide them deep inside her purse, just put them right on top and thought for sure she'd get away with it. That security guard just looked at her like WTH lady and we just died laughing. I'm surprised we all didn't pee our pants. Like who does that, seriously? GP, that's who. Just so ridiculous.

I think we all have that thing, or things, that we'd eat and drink when we went to our grandparents' house. The taste of a refreshing summer drink. The smell of an after-school snack. And don't even get me started on all the things served during the holidays.

At my Grandma and Grandpa Reid's house it's Vernors ginger soda, homage to their home city of Detroit and the only place I drink sodas. At my Grandma Pierce's house it was ants on a log snack (celery topped with peanut butter or cream cheese and raisins) and Orange Julius drinks (orange juice, milk, and vanilla). For my husband, Jeff, it was candies. The kind that he says no one ever actually buys yet the jar is always full. Think: strawberry candies, caramels, and peppermints.

For us, at Grandma Pat's, it was Schwan's frozen food. But let me back this up. Whatever you ate at her home you needed to have the label read first and then a smell test just for good measure because she would keep food for years. And I'm talking about food products a person simply shouldn't keep for that long. Anytime anyone would make any sort of comment about this she'd quickly raise her voice and yell at us that it was fine. She wouldn't force us to eat it but we damn sure better not throw it out while she was watching. Those things were still good, by God!

Back to Schwan's food. I vividly remember looking through the Schwan's catalog making notes and telling my grandma what I wanted to order. It usually included some type of soft pretzels and dessert treat like ice cream cups (or peppermint stick ice cream when in season). To this day when I see that Schwan's truck driving around town, I smile to myself and instantaneously crave a soft pretzel.

One of my favorite quotes from her came from soft pretzels and a game night (more on our family's love for game night later). We were playing Catch Phrase and if you've never played this game, I'll attempt to give a quick explanation.

First, you're divided into two teams and you have an electronic disc to pass around. On that disc, you pick a topic. A word or phrase will pop up and you try to explain it without saying the word to coax your team members to guess the word. Once they guess it, you pass it to the other team. The round continues until the timer runs out at which point, whoever is holding the disc when it buzzes, loses that round and the winning team scores a point. You play until a team reaches seven points.

Well, we must have been on a food topic or snacks of some sorts. When the disc got to grandma the timer was nearly the end. We were all hyped up and her word was pretzel. After giving us a handful of hints, none of them helpful, she yelled in her northern accent, "Well, you can stuff it you know!" And the timer ran out.

She was so mad we didn't know what she was referring to! Her mostly pretend anger quickly turned into tears from laughter. Of all things to say to explain the word pretzel, that's what she went for. But honestly, I should've guessed that!

I went vegetarian and then eventually vegan (not consuming any animal products) at a young age and even though she never quite understood my eating choices or me in general sometimes, she always wanted to and tried to embrace me. When I would visit her, she would make sure the house was stocked with soymilk. Her little olive branch, as to say, "I'm not totally sure what all this veg stuff is about but soymilk is the most obvious and best choice and an easy way to show I'm trying." It's something little but a memory that still means a lot to me.

She wanted everyone to be included at her house. And that didn't only include her family. Everyone was welcome. The mailman? Sure. Your best friend's mom's sister's second cousin on her husband's side? Why not! She always had the house where everyone wanted to be. This was generational, from her kids to grandkids and I'm sure it would have continued with her great-grandchildren as well. Being at her home was altogether fun. I want to be like that. Come one, come all. It's fun to constantly be surrounded by family and friends and then, hey, since you wouldn't often be leaving your house, you never have to get out of loungewear if you don't want to. Sounds good to me.

She would be up later than anyone. She'd gamble with the best of them. Give her all the slot machines please. I don't know many grandparents who would want to come to Las Vegas for their grandchild's 21st birthday but she came for mine. That's who she was. She loved to travel, loved to gamble, and loved to have a good time. Oh, and loved to have some adult beverages. So really, when you think about it, Vegas is a prime spot for her. So off we went together and she had as good of a time as me (the birthday girl), my immediate family, or my cousins.

She would dance the longest at any wedding. Try to picture an elderly woman gently swaying from side to side while her arms moved in an only slightly less enthusiastic manner than Carlton from *The Fresh Prince of Bel-Air*. That pretty much sums up her dance moves. She was never worried, or at least didn't seem to be, about impressing other people, she was only concerned with her family and how we were all doing.

We went on numerous trips together from the Badlands National Park in South Dakota to throughout Italy on a European escapade and all in between.

She was such a character that going on an Italian adventure with her, my mom and stepdad, and one of my best friends, will always be stored under things I will never forget and things I've enjoyed most in my life.

We toured the historic spots with awe and disbelief, ventured out with numerous tour groups and made new buddies, shopped (duh), drank limoncello together, and watched her get hit on and serenaded by an older Italian man. At this time her husband, my Grandpa Chet, has already passed so not to worry about any jealousy there. She laughed and laughed and although this wasn't an episode of the Bachelor, although with the settings we were in, it easily could have been, she accepted the rose he offered. She never admitted she truly thought he was hitting on her even though we looked at her as though she was crazy denying it; it was so clear. And it was all incredible.

We all have seen, as well as probably have been, the people running in the airport to catch their plane. GP was no different. Envision a short and only slightly stout grandma jogging shoeless behind her daughter and granddaughter to catch a plane in Memphis. Yelling loudly and objectively at the situation. As you can imagine, that was in her younger days. As she got older, she would continue yelling at the crappy situation of delayed flights and short connections but would motion us to run. Or, our first choice, we would attempt to flag down a beeping cart with flashing lights to carry us to our gate.

She went on many trips over the years with grandpa and with her family and often to visit her family. With all her travels, what she loved the most in this world was us. Her family. She loved us hard. And ultimately loved so hard that it led to her passing.

My uncle passed away from early onset Alzheimer's and shortly after that she passed away too. I think it was just too much to have to watch your child die. But none of us expected her death. In fact, I think most of us never really thought she'd ever be gone. We were shocked. Of course, we get how things work. People get older and they eventually leave this place for what many of us believe is a better one, but we were all genuinely stunned she was gone. It was hard to comprehend. She was the head of the family and that person isn't ever supposed to give up their place with us. I think in some ways it's how she would've wanted to go. Not slow and painful and lingering on but suddenly because her heart just couldn't take anymore. Dying from a broken heart is a very real thing.

So many lessons can be learned from this woman with the most significant and the greatest being the importance of family. Love them at all times, even when they piss you off like we so often did (the time I got put in the back of a cop car and delivered back to her house when my friends and I were up visiting her for a summer and got into a little trouble with drinking, comes to mind quickly). Love them above anything else. Hold them close and cherish them.

LESSONS LEARNED:

- Cherish family above all else. Put your family first but always have room at your table, home, cabin for friends who are like family. Love those people with all your heart, all the time.
- Eat slowly.
- Unapologetically be yourself.
- Speak up. Be loud. Let your voice be heard.
- Teach your kids and grandkids to make you drinks. Kidding...sort of. Or not.

CHAPTER TWO

HYSTERICAL HUBS

Let me start off by saying I love my husband Jeff.

A friend of mine told me that she thought about the television show *Dharma and Greg* when thinking about Jeff and me. This made me laugh and nod my head in agreement as I pondered this.

Dharma and Greg was the late 1990s sitcom about a couple who are somewhat mismatched yet hit it off and fall in love. Dharma is the eccentric bohemian daughter of hippies and Greg is the son of country-club bluebloods. To a point, this is our story, minus the getting married on the first date part, the parental disapproval, and the abrupt divorce (fingers crossed and Lord willing).

Though I'm a bit of a flower child, I'm way more OCD than Dharma and than Jeff, probably more of a Greg trait. More on being Type A later. We've been together for 12+ years and I really do adore the man.

Don't worry this isn't about to get sappy.

I know he can be an ass. I say this to say that one of his best traits is that he never judges me, or at least doesn't make me feel like he is. He may be somewhat harsh towards people he doesn't know and give his friends shit but he never judges me. He loves my friends as I do. And loves my family just the same.

We fit well. Funny story, really, in regards to him and my family. We met in 2006 when he was training under my mom to become a nursing home administrator. My family has known Jeff's for a while as the company both my mom and stepdad worked for is one that Jeff's father started.

So, when Jeff decided to somewhat follow in his dad's footsteps, his dad decided Mary, my mom (lots more on her later), would be the ideal person to teach him the ropes. Jeff walked in on his first day and said, "I think you're supposed to be my new boss." From that point on she has served as his mentor in work and life. I'm so thankful for that because she is the perfect person to have in that role.

After we met, we continued to see each other around town with our intertwining friend group and then we connected one-on-one when I arrived at the facility in 2008 to work as a volunteer during my senior year of high school. Yeah, he's a handful of years older than I am and was already out of college. We both began working on a project together to recruit new volunteers, which we did (go us!), shortly afterwards started dating, and the rest is history.

We bonded over the hilarity of the show and music of Flight of the Concords. Top hits we'd play on repeat would be "Business Time", "The Most Beautiful Girl", and "I'm Not Crying". If you don't know about Flight of the Concords, do yourself a huge favor and GTS (Google that shit) ASAP.

Laughing pretty much constantly, we instantly knew we were similar in humor and interests and hit it off well.

I left for college at Florida State University shortly after we started dating and we did the long-distance thing for years. That absolutely had its tough moments, but he never minded returning to his alma mater (go 'Noles!). He moved. I moved. We made it all work until eventually we settled into our life together in the Florida Panhandle and the rest is history.

More so than the things I mentioned above and more so than his handsome looks and sweet dance moves, his best trait by far is his sense of humor and ability to make anyone laugh and be at ease.

Admittedly, I am an easy laugh and a sucker for corny jokes but it's not just me or our toddler child whom he makes laugh, although he has been spitting out dad jokes since long before we even thought about having kids.

It's all of those who are around him whom he can entertain and make laugh. But it's not only jokes -- he doesn't go around spitting out knock-knock jokes -- it's the way he makes commonplace things hysterical.

This goes back to when he was a kid. He had a middle school project about the Wright brothers titled, *Two Wrongs Don't Make a Right, But Two Wrights Make an Airplane*. Who thinks of this stuff? He's proud of that one to this day. He also is the only child I've ever heard of getting in trouble for disrespecting Amy Grant, a person who, interestingly enough, I think he probably does respect. I mean, she is a talented little lady.

At his Christian middle school choir practice, Jeff and a buddy were goofing off, as boys that age generally do, especially when they're forced to do something they'd rather not be doing. The director finally had enough of their antics and gave them detention for disrespecting Amy Grant, the artist whose song they were attempting to sing. That's literally what he wrote on their detention slip. Disrespecting Amy Grant. Have you ever heard of such a thing?

He was the kid to test boundaries and be a bit rebellious. Two stories come to mind.

The first is when he and his friend, a known troublemaker, were playing with fire. They were next door to Jeff's house messing around at a lot for a house that was under construction. They had started a fire in a bucket and had the fire contained, until they didn't. The fire got bigger than expected and his friend picked up something nearby, thinking it would put the fire out. What he didn't realize was that he grabbed a piece of black tar paper, which instantly made the fire grow larger, catching the siding of the house on fire. As I said, this was a house being built, and the siding wasn't completed, it still had the plastic siding on it. This burned up in seconds and the fire made its way to the wood.

The boys frantically threw sand and dirt onto the fire until finally, they contained it. They never got caught and it wasn't for many, many years later that Jeff's parents found out. He really dodged a bullet there.

The next story also involves neighbors, but different ones this time. Jeff had a bow and arrow that he couldn't get enough of. One day, he shot an arrow into their neighbors' prickly pear cactus. He fell in love with the thud noise the arrow made when it punctured the cactus' pads. Jeff went to town on that bad boy. I can understand that appeal and satisfaction for sure.

Well, what Jeff didn't realize was that cacti don't heal once they are pierced, and this cactus happened to be about 100 years old. The neighbor was devastated. Jeff's prim and proper Southern belle mother (she's the type of woman you refer to as ma'am, a woman who knows how to fold a fitted sheet, and a woman who cites the Mason-Dixon line as a geographical point of reference) was utterly ashamed. Thoroughly embarrassed. She forced Jeff to march his tail to their home to apologize for the damage he had caused. To this day he feels badly but, he also fondly remembers that noise.

Other random things he does to make every day instances fun is joking around with babies and kiddos of our family or friends. He'll bounce them on his lap helping them flail their arms around to whatever music is playing or scoop them up and run around the house holding them and pretending to dance wildly. Kids love it and adults love to watch. You can't experience the silliness without laughing.

He loves wordplay. He'll see or smell something he knows will be delicious and say something like, "Nom Kippur." He'll be cold and say, "Burrrrberries and cream." Feel free to use either of those for your own merriment and pleasure.

Few days have passed since we've been together that he hasn't made me laugh. Those days were probably wrapped up in some type of fun argument about his leaving hats all over the house or my putting things away in places he can't find them (his words, not mine, as I clearly think they're in the perfectly assigned and logical spot).

I'm a bit, okay a lot, OCD, when it comes to the cleanliness of our home. To Jeff's defense, he went from his mother picking up after him, to then his Type A college roommate, to then, shortly after, having me in his life so he hasn't really been forced to pick up after himself.

He wants things to be organized and orderly, he just doesn't put much thought into doing it himself. From his viewpoint, it's his home, he can do what he wants. From my viewpoint, we're roommates, only now we're married.

Going back to the hat arguments. When we were first living together, I can vividly remember conversation after conversation with him begging him to please put them away. He would forget and I would do it and it would drive me crazy.

If he only had a handful of hats, he probably would pick them up because he would need to know where they were in a few days. But he probably had close to a hundred hats. Now, every time he buys a hat, I make him donate an old one. One simply does not need that many hats.

The same goes with his cups. He always has about five cups out at a time, probably because he misplaces one and then gets a new one and they just add up. He will either leave them all over the house or stacked up in the sink. We have a dishwasher. He's always had a dishwasher. FOR HEAVEN'S SAKE, JUST PUT THEM IN THE DISHWASHER! I don't understand what's so difficult.

I used to wish I was a little crazier and could be the type of person who would put all his hats in a pile outside and light them on fire. But I'm not, so I couldn't. To be honest, the hats and cups don't bother me as much anymore (hey, maybe I'm getting more laidback!) but to his defense, he also has improved some over the years. It is funny, or maybe interesting is a better word, that while he isn't fazed by stacks of paper next to his bedside or leaving his things strewed about the house, he is more rigid about other things.

For example, the way he closes chip bags. My brother Ron opened a bag of tortilla chips while visiting us, and as he unwrapped the bag, he looked at me as to say this must be my doing.

Nope, that's all Jeff. He folds bags as if they are birthday presents to be taped up and given away to a special someone. Very meticulous. Same with kitchen towels. He will precisely fold them before hanging them back up. Even his napkin, regardless if it's clean or dirty, he folds precisely.

Ron is flabbergasted by a similar situation with his wife Anna. Their entire house could be a wreck. A mess. On fire, even. Yet, their bed will be made. The rest of their room will have shoes, clothes, and jewelry all over the place but dammit if that bed won't be properly made with decorative pillows in their rightful place. Sometimes he laughs at this, sometimes he wants to strangle himself with the bedsheets. Marital bliss, am I right?

Jeff's very much a people person and humor and interacting with others comes easily for him. Very natural. I would call myself an outgoing introvert while he is very much an outgoing extrovert. He doesn't like to be alone where I thrive on time to and for myself (having kids takes that away realllll quick). He truly is the definition of an extrovert. Websters would explain an extrovert as an "outgoing, overtly expressive person" and that absolutely sums him up. I tend to call him dramatic, but I guess "overtly expressive" is probably a kinder term. I'll keep that in mind. He's quick-witted and knows how to make light of everything and make anything humorous. He makes up songs about anything.

Some of my favorite moments from college is when he would freestyle using the T-Pain (remember him?!) app about my friends, bringing us to tears we laughed so hard.

Roommate brought someone home from the fraternity house? Yup, that's prime material. Roommate dating someone whose family owns a bagel shop and therefore, she'd get free food? Yeah, that's going to translate into a musical composition. Roommate being a sore loser when her professional football team loses? Yeah, he'll jam out with that as material too.

Throughout the time I've known him he would whip out his guitar whenever friends were over and jam. Give him a topic to make up a song about and he's on it. Not to mention he can hear a song and play it without reading music, a trait he gained from his mother, which is incredible to me. Now he makes up songs about our toddler no longer wearing diapers and remixes "Itsy Bitsy Spider" and nursery rhymes on his guitar, affectionately titling this new genre *Kids Music That Doesn't Suck* (can we please never listen to a song about a family of sharks ever again?!) and it's still just as funny. Less vulgarity but same amount of humor.

Years ago, Jeff randomly began giving the animals in my mom and stepdad's house voices. Casper, the giant black anti-social cat snuck down the stairs and all of a sudden had a narration with the voice of William Shatner.

Otis, the tiny brown hyper Yorkshire Terrier, didn't obtain a specific celebrity alias but rather just a high-strung, fast-talking, high-pitched voice as he ran circles around the living room.

I can't wait to hear the voice our soon-to-be pet fish for

our daughter will have. Regardless if it's a boy or a girl (and does anyone know how you tell that on a fish??), I know it'll be good. These voices of his don't extend only to animals. We pulled into a former mining town in Tennessee on a recent RV trip and he immediately transformed himself into an old prospector like he's Will Ferrell playing Gus Chiggins on *Saturday Night Live*. Maybe his next calling is in animated film narration. If anyone has any connections, I've got the perfect guy for the job.

Along with being the funniest person I know, he's uber well-rounded. Take a smart, handsome, faith-based, athlete who's also musically talented, and there you have him. While he is all of those wonderful things, there are things that he is not.

He is the type who, while he likes to fix things and solve problems, he isn't what I would call "handy". He isn't going to renovate a house or spend lots of time in a man shed, he'd rather pay someone to do things like that, which I can totally respect. But now give him a golf club to fix and that he has covered. Or give him a man cave with multiple televisions to watch sports on and he's a happy camper.

Speaking of campers, he loves being outside but don't ask him to go camping and sleep on the ground, he's not that rugged but he will 'glamp' with the best of them. Explore trails, streams, outside in general? Yes. Sleep in a tent? No. Also, he is not good at dealing with small or enclosed spaces. Yeah, planes aren't his thing.

He's a classic guy. A bit old school in some ways. He'd choose singing from a hymnal over contemporary Christian songs at church. "Silver Bells" by Bing Crosby will forever be his favorite Christmas song. But despite being a classic guy, you'll only catch him reading electronic books. No physical books for him. He hates, I mean loathes, touching paper. Money doesn't count (no pun intended). Me, I love the feeling of holding a book, turning the pages, the way libraries smell. For him, not so much. He doesn't understand that sentiment. I've heard of people having a disinterest in touching cardboard, but I don't think I can recall meeting anyone other than him who doesn't like touching paper. Strange phobia.

I mentioned he was handsome, but as we all do, he went through some interesting looks over the years, even getting his ears pierced. When Jeff was in middle school, which means his older sister was in high school, his family took a trip to the Bahamas. They returned with sun-glowing skin and matching puka shell necklaces but while they were down there, they snapped a picture of the two of them. Now keep in mind that this was the 1990s so the pukas were in and so were small framed sunglasses. Anyway, they practically were matching with their accessories and looks and to top it off, their hair. They both have curly, curly hair. Jeff went through a phase of wanting his long. The long and the short of this little story is that he and his sister ended up looking like lesbian lovers in this picture.

Jeff continued this longer curly hair look through his senior year, so his high school graduation portrait looks like he has an afro. It's amazing. If you want a visualization of what his sister looked like growing up, just conjure up (or do a quick internet search for) the portrait of Amy Grant on her 1980s *A Christmas Album* cover. That's pretty much her.

Have you heard of the ancient "art" of foot binding? If so, you can skip forward a few sentences, if not, let me explain. Foot binding began in China in about the 10th century believed to be by a dancer who was altering her foot to the shape of a new moon. It was a tradition that consisted of breaking and fastening girls' feet to change their shape and size. Smaller feet were deemed to be more glamorous and beautiful than "normal" sized feet, making them a status symbol. What I'm about to make a comparison to and make jokes about truly started as a painful process and a desolate, sad time in Chinese history.

Okay, so now that you know a little bit about the history of foot binding, let me tell you where Jeff comes into play with this. When I first met him and up until about five years ago, he was wearing size 10 shoes. Jeff, in reality, wears a size 11 or 11.5. He was wondering why his feet hurt and why his pinky toes were starting to get blisters and calluses. He just had it in his head that he was a size 10. Who knows how long before I met him that he was doing this?

It wasn't until I brought to his attention that he was practically, although inadvertently, binding his feet and he should probably look into measuring his feet. That day we got out a piece of printer paper and I measured his foot and of course it was nowhere near a 10 anymore. He went to the shoe store to get a measurement from an expert. As we suspected, he was indeed not a size 10.

Jeff's face is a magnet for cuts and scars. He went through a period where he was constantly hurting himself in some way and ending up with a scar on his face. But before that run in his life of constant bad facial luck, his initial scar story dates back to when he was in first grade. The class was doing some sort of fun activity and had their desks pushed together. Jeff tried to get up to do something and his foot got caught in his backpack and he couldn't catch himself on anything and then, ouch! He busted his chin open.

Fast forward throughout his childhood and I'm sure he had a handful more, but his adult scar stories begin during a round of Dizzy Bat at his fraternity house at Florida State University. When reading these things, you probably assume the obvious that this will not end well. Well, that's the same feeling I had when he was telling me this story.

Dizzy Bat, for one. Frat house, for two. There's literally zero chance this story wouldn't end in either something hysterical happening or someone getting hurt or in this case, both. So, he and his buddies are busy playing what I can only imagine is a competitive game of Dizzy Bat (I just assume that everything at a fraternity house is competitive). What's Dizzy Bat, you ask? Well, although somewhat self-explanatory, I had never heard of it either but it's a drinking game in which the participant chugs a full beer out of a Wiffle ball bat while the bystanders count how long it takes for the participant to finish the beer. Then, the participant leans over to put his forehead on the end of the bat and spins around the number of times equal to the number of seconds it took to finish the beer. The participant then gets his beer can tossed in the air so he can attempt to hit the can. If he doesn't, he must spin more and try again. If he still doesn't hit the ball, the crowd probably throws the beer can directly at him.

While I think this sounds humorous to watch, it's not the first game I personally would sign up to play. Okay, so now that the rules are sorted out, back to the story. Jeff chugs his beer, does his spinning, hits the can (star athlete, my man) and then decides it's smart to run as if he's a Major League Baseball player. It is then when he stumbles and his face makes contact with the brick wall. Gushing blood and, unbeknownst to him, the first of a handful of facial scars during his young adult life.

The next scar story again takes place during college. Jeff and some friends decided to go to south Florida for New Year's Eve. This, AGAIN, I just shake my head at because the idea of a bunch of fraternity boys in South Florida for any holiday just seems like it will end in someone getting arrested or hurt or just something going wrong.

In this case, it was more of a wrong place at the wrong time situation as it turns out it actually wasn't the fault of Jeff or any of his buddies. Someone they knew had started a fight inside the club they were at, unbeknownst to Jeff and his friends who were outside trying to hail a cab. This acquaintance broke a bottle and tried to stab someone with it. Class act, I know. The fight grew bigger and bigger, gaining more people and momentum until it spilled out of the club and onto the streets. It was there that Jeff turned around just to get sucker punched by a guy who was holding a lighter. Jeff and his friends tried to escape the situation as quickly as they could but the scar on his temple remains to this day.

When you're a newbie in a company, paying your dues, the owner's son, and single without kids, you often get placed in the area few people would voluntarily choose. Cue Jeff's first gig after his administrator-in-training role with my mom. Straddling the Mississippi/Alabama border, Jeff worked as an interim administrator in one little town and resided in another (due to more room at the inn). He was living in a hotel and his dinner options consisted of either a fast-food restaurant or a diner. The fast-food joint being the scene of a recent shooting.

Jeff was settling into his new role and wanted to go into work early to meet the night shift team. His alarm went off before the sun came up. Hopping out of bed, he began his morning routine. He drank some water and then opened a Diet Coke to start caffeinating his body. This was before he discovered the delicious goodness known as coffee but that's neither here nor there. He gives his diet drink a big chug and it's then his morning goes awry. For some reason the liquid is having a difficult time making its way from mouth to stomach. This triggers his body into having some sort of spasm and BAM! He falls to the ground in the bathroom, hitting his face on the toilet on the way down, passing out cold. When he wakes up, the sun is also up. He's dazed and confused. He wraps himself up in a towel (he was preparing to shower before this all went down) and stumbles to the front desk. He's bleeding all over the place and attempting to tell them what happened and ask for help. Of course, being a little leery after the recent nearby shooting, the staff was nervous at first but when they realized this wasn't a crime scene or dangerous situation, they were quick to call for help. He was rushed to a hospital in a larger city nearby where he stayed for a few days of tests. Turns out Jeff's heart went into atrial fibrillation, or AFib for short, which is a type of heart arrhythmia. The irregular beating of the heart can interrupt normal blood flow and cause a plethora of problems. After being the youngest of his friends and acquaintances to wear a heart monitor and hearing many jokes, he was cleared to go back to life as normal with nothing to worry about except another scar on his face.

A large byproduct for many of us who attended Florida

State University is a love for football. And with that often follows a love for tailgating. One gameday weekend Jeff was hosting some friends of his and some of mine at his house. The day started off with Jeff and a buddy playing and winning a golf tournament. They were elated but little did they know where this day would take them.

Other than pride, their tournament winnings consisted of a large trophy. This trophy served as their shared chalice that they proceeded to drink their beverages from throughout the day as if it were a medieval goblet, filled with a magic potion. In reality, it was filled with some type of light beer.

The day continued with outdoors games and grilling food at Jeff's house, along with televising the football game. It was an away game so we, of course, had to pretend like we were all at the game and have as much fun as we would if everything was in person. One of my girlfriends and I, along with one of his buddies, were all planning to stay the night there, so I had my overnight bag in his room.

Let me interrupt this story and say that foolishly, the buddy he golfed with thought it would be okay to chance the drive back to his house about three hours away. Well, he got onto the interstate and then off at the next exit, deciding it'd be best to check his ass into the nearest hotel. Good effort. Say no to drinking and driving, especially when you can have a slumber party with friends.

Anyway, the night came to an end and it was time for bed. I drift off to sleep but suddenly I'm startled by a loud noise. BANG! Jeff had somehow stumbled to where my suitcase was and tripped over it when he woke up to use the restroom. It was nowhere near his path so it's almost like he had to sleepwalk out of his way to run into my bag. Instead of falling on the floor and banging up his knees or something like that, his face, of course, finds his dresser. He hits right above his eyebrow and it is gushing blood.

In his tired and mad state, he was refusing to get help, but we outnumbered him and insisted he needed to go to the emergency room. We very much assumed he would need stitches. So, we all hopped in an Uber together for our late-night joyride to the ER. We were right. He did need stitches. About nine or so of them actually. And unfortunately, he now has another scar story to tell. Truly, his life sometimes reminds me of a slapstick comedy show.

Okay, so one final facial scar story hopefully for the rest of his lifetime, knock on wood.

This story involves night putting. Now, most of you, like myself, hear the words night putting and just understand that there's no way for this story to end but in disaster. Okay, so Jeff went on a golf trip to practically middle of nowhere, Georgia with some of his guy friends. After golfing from dawn until dusk, they still hadn't had enough so they decided to grab a lantern and some brews and venture out onto the course to practice their putts.

Now, I don't know if you have much experience with true golf addicts but that's what these boys are. Addicts. They can never get enough and it sometimes gets in the way of their better judgement. Okay, so, onto the course they go. All is going fine, until Jeff's buddy, while walking backwards as he watches his putt hopefully enter the hole, trips over the lantern. Picture this is slow motion: Jeff is extending his hand to try to catch him while the putter, still in his buddy's hand, is quickly ascending upward in an attempt for him to try to catch himself. Well, as Jeff's facial luck would have it, the putter makes contact right above his eye (thank God it missed his actual eye) and he once again finds himself gushing blood from his face. They pack up their things and head to the house they're staying at to assess the damage. The buddy who Jeff was attempting to help is a bit of a shitshow and loose cannon. He was also highly intoxicated. I say this lovingly because he is also hysterical but also so you get an understanding of who he was dealing with. His buddy insists he doesn't need stitches and he can just sleep it off. Jeff, who probably sobered up a bit after seeing his life flash before his eyes, is thinking a little clearer and tells his buddy to pretty much go eff off and that he was going to the emergency room.

Now, remember when I said they were in the middle of nowhere? Well, when I say that, do you picture an award-winning hospital? No, of course not. But the facial Gods were looking out for Jeff during this moment and the one plastic surgeon in the area happened to be the doctor on call. Jeff got stitches and you can barely notice the evidence.

Now I don't want you to think that Jeff is constantly drinking and getting himself into ridiculous, and often painful, situations. It just happens that when there is drinking involved, usually the craziness follows closely behind.

To change the subject, as I mentioned earlier, Jeff is a social butterfly. He doesn't like to be alone. He thrives off the energy of others. He's vocal. Loud. Good relationships thrive on balance between two people, right? He's never met a conversation he didn't want to have. A sport he didn't want to watch. A debate he didn't want to win. Oh, I didn't mention that: he's also very competitive. And he has reason to be that way. He's so freaking good at so many things it's pretty damn disgusting. When I compete, it's with myself. I grew up playing some sports, but dance was my thing (ballerina for 15+ years, holla). If Jeff can compete at something against someone else either in a group or solo setting, he's doing it. It can be something active, like sports, or something unenergetic, like making bets. Either way, he wants in and he wants to be the best. I won't say he's arrogant, although I have (sorry babe), but he believes he can be the best and strives to be at everything he does; even if that's just getting the last word in an argument.

While this has gotten him into some trouble, as you could imagine, it's also boded well for him in his professional life. There's not a job he's interviewed for that he didn't think he'd dominate, and that type of confidence is important. A respectable and admirable way to carry oneself. That coupled with the fact he doesn't overthink things is really a win for him. I, on the other hand, will overthink and overanalyze the shit out of things. There really isn't a situation over the years where I haven't but I'm working on letting him rub off on me and focus on being simply analytical and dropping the 'over' part.

Because Jeff can't or won't or refused to be mediocre at anything, he decided that his first time singing karaoke would be to one of the hardest and fastest songs someone could pick. Think for a second about a very popular song that you've heard. Think late 1980s to early 1990s. Billy Joel. Okay, I'll tell you. It was "We Didn't Start the Fire". Now even if you're a fast reader and can read the words on the screen, you still must know the song fairly well to execute this tune without getting booed off stage. Well in typical Jeff fashion, he hopped up on stage at a place called the Lookout Lounge on the beach in Port St. Joe, Florida. Rest in peace to this little dive bar that got destroyed during Hurricane Michael. I believe my brother Ron was singing backup, i.e., there for moral support while holding a microphone, and jammed out as if he had sung this tune to an audience many times before. Like who does that?? First time singing karaoke I probably went with "No Scrubs" by TLC or something slow and silly. Hmm, now I'm actually really trying to recall what my first karaoke song was. Maybe a Backstreet Boys or

Prince or a Destiny's Child little ditty? It does make me wonder how many times he sang that song in the bathroom watching himself in the mirror for his adoring audience of one. Let me make it clear that I think "We Didn't Start the Fire" is a great song, great song. But I just would never think it should or could be the song one rips off their singing on a stage in front of a crowd of people Band-Aid to. Ah, "I Wanna Dance with Somebody" by Whitney Houston, that had to be my first karaoke song. Good tune, good tune. Interestingly enough, more on that song later.

LESSONS LEARNED:

- Be kind to your spouse or partner, or any of your loved ones for that matter, and don't judge. Be their biggest cheerleader.
- Be as well-rounded as you can. The chicks (and I'm assuming the guys) dig it.
- Be competitive with yourself and/or others to push yourself further and to be your very best.
- Don't be afraid to be silly. Pretend to be a dolphin in a pool, dance with small kids at weddings, and/or give voices to animals you see, etc.

CHAPTER THREE

OXYMORONIC BRO

Have you ever met someone who is put together yet a complete mess all at once? It's incredible. Truly amazing.

Meet my brother Ron. Ron and I are 10 years apart but best friends. Let me rewind a little bit and tell you about my family and how it all came to be.

My parents, Robert and Mary, met in the Peace Corps. Mary was living in Jamaica and Robert was in the Dominican Republic and they sat next to each other at a conference in Washington D.C. If you have a visual of two hippies, that's probably not too far off from the real thing. Anyway, they met, fell in love, got married, and eventually had me.

But prior to all that going down, my dad was living and working in Fiji where he met his first wife and they had my brothers, Ron and Sonny (who also will be talked about soon, just you wait). After they split, their birth mother was no longer in the picture and my mom adopted them. That's how I got so lucky as to grow up with two older brothers. Sorry, not lucky, blessed really.

Robert and Mary eventually broke it off and each remarried but my brothers and I will always be. When people ask about my family and try to put it into certain boxes or put certain labels on it and say "half-brothers" vs "biological" and blah, blah, yadda, yadda, all that, I quickly shoo off that conversation. They are my brothers. Period. Anyway, as you may guess, we don't look much alike. In fact, I can't count the number of times we've been out in a group and people look at Ron and then at me and assume we are together or something along those lines (which makes me silently throw up a bit inside).

Anyway, now that we've run through a brief family history, let's get back to Ron.

Ron is the mediator, middleman, and middle child. He can see all sides of a situation. He's levelheaded. He's been my protector for many years. He's the guy who's run a variety of multimillion-dollar businesses who got fired for going to Burning Man (look it up if you don't know what Burning Man is). All for the best in that situation because one of his simultaneously best and worst traits is that he's loyal. And in that case, if he hadn't gotten fired, he would've kept chugging along in a place where he wasn't meant to be.

He's smart, fun, funny, well-rounded, basically most of the good traits that I mentioned before about Jeff, which is why they probably get along so well. Minus him being as vocal, i.e., loud, as Jeff, which makes for a good balance.

He likes to fix things. Come in, run a business, work out the kinks, help bridge the gaps and then do it again at another place. He is very much a people person. People like him, trust him, support him, and want to work hard for him. He just has a way with people and he is fascinated by them and how our brains work and why people do the things they do. This is a bit of a chicken and egg situation.

He has a master's degree in psychology but if I had to guess, I'd say those interests and fascinations came long before the degree. Or maybe not, he doesn't usually like to be too introspective and talk about himself. He'll listen and help people solve their own problems all day long. But his own? Nah. He certainly does not express his emotions easily or openly. To this day, one of the sweetest cards he's given me was one I received for a recent birthday that has Snoopy on the front that says something along the lines of that everyone should have a sister like me but so far, I'm one-of-a-kind and he closes it saying he loves me and feels so lucky to have me in his life. That is a perfect example of the extent of his illustration of love and feelings. Part silly as to not be too overly sentimental and part sweet and loving and kind. He comes by it honestly though.

Our pops isn't one who likes to discuss feelings, although he has gotten better as he's gotten older. He now ends each phone call by saying he loves us, but still, don't ask him to chit-chat about past situations and how they made him feel or what he loves most about his kids or anything like that.

Ron isn't the guy who is often trying to intentionally make people laugh, yet I'm constantly cracking up at him or his ridiculousness. Probably because he makes light of most situations. As I mentioned, he lets things roll off his back. Take, for example, getting fired.

I remember being in the parking lot of my bank, sitting in my car when he called me and told me his news. Now, we don't chit-chat on the phone so if I see his name come across the screen, I answer. He casually asked me what I was doing. I told him. I then cautiously asked him the same. He said he was sitting at a bar and grill having himself a morning drink. It was before noon and a weekday, so I clearly knew that something was up. He then proceeded to tell me what happened. And just like that, he licked his wounds and went onto the next.

He still makes light of that situation with a sort of eff it attitude but not in an ugly way, more of the attitude of what's done is done and now onto the next thing. Nothing to do now but move on and might as well have a good attitude about it rather than being consumed by the negatives. It's a good trait for me to take from him. Move on. Don't obsess.

There are times when he does play into his easy audience in me. He'll send me memes that he knows would only make me laugh because they are that corny. Ones like, "Did you know Yoda's last name was Layheehoo?" Or recently, we were on a family vacation and discussing turtles at the breakfast table. How we got started talking about this, who knows. The random shit that comes up when we are all together is pretty hysterical. We were talking about turtles protecting themselves with their shells. Maybe we were trying to teach the kids some type of lesson about wildlife or Mother Nature since we were in the mountains surrounded by lots of animals. Probably not though. My guess was this conversation was much more random and less educational than that. Then, Anna asks, "Well how do snapping turtles defend themselves if they can't retract into their shells?" Ron chimes in, "Well it's a good thing they have Ninja Turtles to protect them." Then covers his mouth immediately and goes, "OOOOOOO!" Crowning himself king of the best joke of the day. I'm practically rolling on the floor at this point, dying laughing.

He is pretty much equal parts polished as he is a shit show. Let me give you an example.

I've mentioned my family ties in healthcare and Ron is a part of that as well. Each year there is an annual educational healthcare conference held. Now let me preface this by saying that this conference is also equal parts polished as it is a shit show, so this was really destined to be a perfect storm.

This conference is a place where people vacation with or without their families and have a good ole time while getting educational credits. So, at said conference, Ron decides to hit the hotel lobby bar early with our mom and a group of the usual healthcare suspects. Mom then heads to bed and tries to tag Jeff in to rope Ron into calling it a night. Jeff then fails at proceeding to redirect him and instead they both get wasted and Ron is prancing around trying to take his shirt off. Next day, wheeling and dealing in a suit, feeling fine, flying high like nothing happened. Fast forward to the conference the following year where Ron and his time and time again partner-in-crime, Jeff, decide to once again hit the hotel bar where a woman approaches Ron stating how familiar he looked. She asked if they had met before and swears, he looks just like this guy who last year tried to kiss her at this same conference. Ron of course plays it off, but chances are high he was that guy. This is me laughing, rolling my eyes, and shaking my head.

Let me tell you another little story. Ron was living in the Florida Panhandle on the beach and decided it was time to finally take the plunge and buy some jet-skis for him and his family. Did his research, analyzed the entire situation, found some gems and bought two. He got a great deal! He was so excited. Finally, he and his wife can ride off into the sunset off the coast of the white beaches, wind blowing through his newly inserted hair plugs. They'd escape reality and live their beachgoer's dream. Welp, unfortunately, as it would turn out the title didn't go through. They. Were. Stolen. No wonder he got such a good deal. Looking back and reflecting on the situation and wondering how he could have known or where it could have gone wrong, maybe the telltale sign was that he was trying to buy them off Craigslist. Knick-knacks or smaller items or cheaper items like lawnmowers or other random junk, I mean goods, sure. But higher dollar investment items? No, I don't think I would recommend someone using that platform. And also, now after watching the Lifetime movie, *The Craigslist Killer*, I can't not think about that.

Ron doesn't get hungover. Unlike me, who all it takes is practically the smell of alcohol to get me drunk and then almost simultaneously hungover. I don't know how many of you have been hungover, but Lord knows I've suffered my fair share (read between the lines: too many). They are awful. Pretty much almost the worst thing imaginable. Even one is too many to ever go through. He can stay up nearly all night and then wake up, go for a run, and feel fine. I would be hanging onto the toilet all day and then if I was able to eat anything would need, as Jeff calls it, Vitamin G, which is grease. Greasy foods. Junk food.

Anyway, we were talking one day, about who knows what, and he was commenting that he just can't gain weight and he doesn't get hungover. I think he honestly was saying it as if it was such a problem to have. Poor, pitiful him. What an ass. Thank you, Ron, most of us only wish we had those "problems".

While we are discussing weight gain, let's jump into his eating habits. He grew up an incredible athlete, even gaining an athletic scholarship for college for his baseball skills, and still is, so he's used to being in shape and, as many boys and men, able to mostly eat whatever he wants.

Now that he's entered his 40s I don't know if things will change and of course even though I'm jealous, the kind

OXYMORONIC BRO

part of me hopes it doesn't change for him. Anna and I have helped him eat healthier over the years and I will give him the credit and praise he deserves. He has come a long way, but old habits are hard to break. One of his favorite foods is a hot dog. These can be gourmet, organic, grass-fed, all of the 'healthier' things or simply gas station hot dogs -- he doesn't discriminate. I know you, like myself, wondered for many years who are the people who eat gas station taquitos and hot dogs, well now you at least know one of them.

Actually, taking it a step further and even more disgusting, it was a late Friday evening and Ron and a buddy were at a gas station getting gas and presumably beer and snacks when they overheard that the station attendant was getting ready to throw the hot dogs and other food that's been there for at least a day. They looked at each other and nodded and ended up, in their minds and in their terms, 'scoring' these hot dogs for free. All the leftovers. I'm sure they went to bed as well as woke up with tummy troubles. He brags, if that's the appropriate word, that he lacks working taste buds. Well, in my mind, if this is the case, why not eat super healthy and be the epitome of superior nutrition and be as fit as possible? But, no, he doesn't think like that. He'd rather indulge in the treats that are hot dogs. He also can easily eat an entire pizza by himself. Same thing with the dogs, he can get the organic meat and cheese pizza or simply whatever the nastiest pizza is you can think of and he's satisfied either way.

I will attempt to applaud that he does add in the healthier versions these days though. Eat junk food but make it less awful for you. Ron likes to do this thing in which he calls "shocking the system". What is this exactly, you ask? I'll tell you. He basically will eat what he thinks is ultra-healthy (think spinach, quinoa, and tuna) for about a week and then eat uber unhealthy (think large Blizzards from Dairy Queen, multiple combo meals from McDonald's, etc.). He says he likes to keep his body on its toes. I'm fairly positive he's probably doing more harm than good, but he can't be talked out of it.

He has some other interesting quirks too.

I'm not sure if he's just old school or what but he feels the need to download all of his music. He doesn't trust any of these streaming services; he must own it and dammit if that doesn't come in handy when you have no cell phone service and no downloaded playlists and want to jam. Don't tell him I said that though. I refuse to let him win that battle and stop giving him shit, being that I am very much on the side of the streaming services in this fight.

At least he isn't still carrying around a boombox, Walkman, or CD player so he can tangibly have a grasp on his music (Ron, don't get any ideas here). Remember that though? Look how far our musical technology has come in such a short period of time.

I remember going on a trip up north, to, where else, but North Dakota, and leaving ALL my CDs on the plane. The overwhelming sadness and heartache I felt when I realized what I had done was enough to put anyone into a mental dark hole for sure. Sure, I could buy some of those CDs again but some of those, most of those, were mixes I, or my friends, burned, via illegal outlets, I'm sure. And that's a time-consuming process. Luckily, my cousin gave me some of his CDs to fly home with so I wouldn't be sitting in silence or simply listening to the sound of my own tears. But his music wasn't the same as having my own. Ah, to be able to quickly make a playlist now and carry it with you wherever you go without the heaviness, literally and figuratively, of CDs.

Back to Ron. He also needs to be uber stimulated at almost all times. Ever since I can remember he likes to listen to music with the television on. It bothered me when we were younger, and it drives me effing crazy now. He also rarely listens to an entire song. Maybe I inherited this from him, because I too, cannot, okay, will not, listen to a full song. This is why mashup songs (songs that mix, or mash, more than one song together in case you hadn't heard that term before) and artists like Girl Talk are my jam. Pun intended.

I can vividly remember listening to cassette tapes in his white, 1980s Toyota Corolla, when we were living in Podunk, Arkansas in the 1990s. This was a car in which he had to turn off the air conditioning to get more power to the engine when going uphill, which is somewhat concerning because we lived on dirt roads and up some sketchy hills and in the winter when they would ice over it would be pretty dangerous. I can specifically remember listening to Ace of Base (such a great band) and Genuwine (not quite a one-hit wonder but not anywhere comparable to the caliber of Ace of Base). It wasn't until only about a handful of years ago, when I really listened to Genuwine's hit song, "Pony", and realized how utterly inappropriate that is to listen to with your brother. "If you're horny, let's do it. Ride it, my pony". Seriously, barf. BARF. But I'm sure he knew I couldn't understand what it meant back then but now that I do I cringe a little bit thinking we were anywhere near each other listening to that song.

Back to not listening to one song all the way through though. To skip songs back then, it wasn't easy like it is now. You had to be committed to wanting to change the song to deal with the holding down of the fast-forward button on the tape but dammit, he'd do it. He'd commit. So, while I most likely got some of my eclectic music taste from him, I believe I also received my song ADD from him as well. Let me make a point that the skipping doesn't only occur with songs we don't like. It's songs we love. We just don't want to listen to the entire thing. It's funny because Ron may be slightly ADD or ADHD, but I'm really the opposite. I am rarely impulsive. I mean, I told you about my preference for and ability to overanalyze damn near everything. Some quirks, as with this one, don't need reasoning, they are merely inherited and passed down to others.

Continuing on the topic of cars. Ron taught me how to

drive a stick shift in his early 2000s blue Mustang. That car was his baby at the time so it's somewhat surprising he entrusted me with this prized possession. But that's Ron. No sweat, no worries. Cool, calm, and collected and I suppose this situation was no different. I would not be the same. I'm nervous when even my husband drives me around and he's been driving for over 20 years. Maybe Ron thought it would be fun. Maybe he knew I wouldn't be a speed racer and ruin anything or anyone if we crashed. Either way, he taught me, and it was fun. Afterward, I didn't rush out to place a car with a manual transmission on my wishlist for my first ride, or any car I've had, but I can see the appeal for sure.

Whether he has zero beers or 10, and I'm only saying that to reference that it's not a drunken sloppy thing, he loves sleeping on the floor. And I don't mean carpet, he prefers hardwood, like his inherited through marriage dog, Grover. It's very odd.

He also loses a shoe, yes, singular, as in one, at least a couple times per year. They are usually flip-flops, which of course make them easier to randomly fall off one's foot, but I still am at a loss how it actually happens. I wish I could have a video crew follow him around sometimes to catch all his shenanigans on tape and solve the mysteries of how these things happen. Is he kicking something and it flings off? Does he simply walk out of it and keep going, not noticing it ever happened? I need to know these things!

Sometimes it makes me and Anna crazy that he is or wants to be friends with everyone but honestly, it's a good trait to have. He's never judgmental of anyone and can find a way to relate to every person he meets. He truly lives by the 'be curious, not judgmental' mentality and is always welcoming. He embraces diversity, a trait he was presumably born with.

He is destined for greatness. Actively, currently on his way to it now, I believe. You can now find him at the Piggly Wiggly (yes, those are a thing and yes, they still exist here in the south) slinging groceries and making sandwiches (not really, well, except when they're short-staffed) and helping his father-in-law buy up all the grocery stores in the southeast and have total grocer domination. And when he isn't working, you'll find him playing sports, teaching their kids not to be assholes (Ron and Anna's choice of words and life goals, not something I made up), and on his way to making millions.

LESSONS LEARNED:

- Embrace everyone. Make friends with anyone.
- Remain cool, calm, and collected even under pressure and brush things off easily.
- Don't be afraid to look inward to try to understand your feelings or your hurts or your struggles.
- Don't buy jet-skis or other high-priced items off Craigslist.
- Carry extra shoes in case one magically falls off your foot

and happens to go missing.

CHAPTER FOUR

WILD CARD BROTHER

And now let's talk for a little while about my oldest brother, Sonny, shall we?

Sonny has always marched to his own drum. We lovingly call him our family's wild card. He's unpredictable. I don't mean this in a dangerous or threatening way, as if he's going to pull a shiv out on you, but more of a humorous statement as in you never know what he's going to wind up doing next. That's the thing about Sonny, he's very sneaky. He'll do things and you either won't even know what he's getting you into or what he's doing. And honestly, the more I think about it, although he's very smart (more on that later) maybe he, himself, doesn't even realize when he's being sneaky. He's a bit spacey. Like the time he decided it would be a good idea to smoke pot in the limo after our mom got remarried. It was no big deal to him and when we all realized what he was doing and told him he clearly couldn't do that inside, he just looked at us not understanding the big deal. A look on his face as to say, "What? Doesn't everyone do this?"

Before I came along, my family lived in the Dominican Republic. While living there they had a nanny or housekeeper or whatever the best term is for someone who helped out around the house.

Help there was inexpensive, but this woman came with a little bit of baggage. She liked to drink. A lot. I'm not sure if this is what caused what I'm about to tell you or not, but it probably didn't help. Apparently, she made the worst sandwiches known to mankind. We aren't talking gourmet or any type of complicated sandwich; we're just talking about a good ole fashioned peanut butter and jelly sandwich. How you can mess up a PB&J so that a child doesn't want to eat it, I will never know but that's how bad they were.

So, she would make these sandwiches for Ron and Sonny for school and neither of them would eat them. Ron would trade them with his classmates for other food, but Sonny would always forget to do something with his until he got home (not sure what he would eat for lunch but in typical Sonny form, he got by somehow and never went hungry). He'd arrive back to the house and open his backpack and chuck his sandwich under the tangerine tree outside the house. Well, after quite the stack piled up, our dad finally saw them and Sonny was busted. Now, our dad is a garbage disposal. He's not heavy or overweight by any means, he just hates wasting food and would constantly eat any leftover food on our plates. This was probably due to the fact he has spent lots of his time working in a variety of Third World countries and knows that many people in poverty can't afford to fill their bellies. I think this stuck with him (even to this day). So needless to say, he was not happy when he saw all this food that wasn't eaten.

Another thing Sonny used to do with his food he disliked while at the dinner table would be to hide it. Well, he didn't really hide it so much as just drop it under his chair and thought or hoped it would disappear. We didn't have dogs, nor does he have superpowers to make it disappear, but this is another trait of his that will be a reoccurring theme. He has the mentality that if he ignores it, it'll just go away.

One food that Sonny never let go to waste was ice cream. He couldn't get enough of it. He would get out a bowl and fill it to the top. Now, I'm not talking about a regular bowl for salad or soup. I'm talking about a mixing bowl. He would pile on scoop after scoop and then add any and every topping he could scavenge from the fridge or pantry and finish it all. I have no doubt he could polish off a half gallon all by himself. He still does this to this day when it's available.

Sonny is honest. He can't or won't lie. Ask him a question and he will straight-up tell you the truth, even if it's something he shouldn't have done or something you may not like the answer to. He'll just be honest. An admirable trait for sure.

Growing up both my brothers were star athletes, as I mentioned briefly about Ron, and they specifically thrived in basketball and baseball. Even though they were separated by a couple years, they would often be on the same teams. You may think, well, since Ron is younger, he must have been the better athlete to end up being on the same team as his older brother and maybe that's true, but another truth is that Sonny wasn't quite what many, or at least Ron, would call coachable.

One day during a varsity basketball game in high school, Ron was playing and Sonny was on the bench while their mutual friend was giving Sonny crap for not being on the court when his younger brother was. So finally, their friend had egged Sonny on enough to convince him he should tell their coach that he should be in the game. Sonny gets the nerve to call out to the coach and their friend thinks he's really going to let the coach know what he's feeling. Instead, what does Sonny do? He yells out, "Coach!" When the coach turns around, Sonny just waves at him and goes back to his seat.

He'll speak his mind, but confrontation is not his thing. He's fairly timid for the most part. Another coach and athletic story our mom tells about Sonny goes as follows.

Let me begin by saying that our mom was not a helicopter parent who would yell in the coach's ear to put her kid into the game. She respected the boundaries and let everyone have their rightful place in it all. But one day, she was feeling a bit perturbed so she pulled the basketball coach aside to chat with him. She told the coach that she felt Sonny was really a great player and a strong athlete and she was wondering why he didn't play during games more often. The coach quickly agreed that Sonny was an excellent player, however, he also said that when Sonny gets really into the game, they never know what hoop he will score in. Will it be for his own team? Will it be for their opponent? He gets so into playing that he doesn't see clearly or coherently. Oh, Sonny.

While Sonny is definitely book smart, he's not really what one would call street smart. People like this always crack me up. Not to get too off topic but I have a friend from high school who is so spacey. I thought for the longest she was such a ditz. I say that lovingly and so would her best friends. But homegirl is now a Certified Registered Nurse Anesthetist so she clearly has brains. I'm not saying that I'd want her putting me to sleep, but I'm saying she legally can.

Anyway, back to Sonny. He is very much like that, just our own little space cadet. In elementary school he even skipped a grade. In hindsight it may have been best to keep him where he was until his maturity level matched his academic level. But, then again, the mismatched maturity levels are often the case with boys so what can you do?

Now when I say smart, I don't just mean run-of-the-mill smart, I mean really smart. Top of your class smart. That was him. Notice I said was. Past tense. He did not graduate from high school at the top of his class because when you're a wild card you live by your own rules. He never gave an eff. I don't mean that rude or unruly, he just always did his own thing and never worried (even when maybe he should have a little) about what people thought. Including our parents. So yes, while he could've graduated top of his class, he decided he was just over it. He had a French class project his senior year that he just didn't do. When he makes up his mind, he's done. There's no convincing him to finish. He's simply done. My folks may think otherwise, but I think there is something respectable in that. Maybe not when you're a kid and you don't really know better and probably should be listening to older, more mature people, but as you get older, not being swayed to go against your own convictions is a good trait to have.

Despite not completing his French class final project, he graduated more than fine, achieving an academic scholarship, and went onto college. Where he ended up dropping out. Twice. Again, can't be controlled or told what to do. Doesn't give an eff.

Sonny moved to Northern California, deciding he wanted to live off the land, a theme that will continue throughout his life. After a solid attempt at this endeavor -- I honestly don't know the exact time and he wouldn't remember such minute things -- that situation wasn't panning out and he was hungry. Well, I certainly have been hangry before and it sure does make us not think straight. To this point, he clearly was not of sound mind.

He decides he is going to go to a nearby small town and rob a bank. Armed only with a wooden staff, he hides out in the bathroom until everyone is gone. Why a wooden staff? Well, he either went full Biblical and hoped it would give him some type of divine power or it was the only weapon he could afford (read: he made it and it was free). I'm guessing the latter. So, when everyone left for the day, he comes out, sees the safe but then he realizes he is locked in.

Let's analyze the safe for a second. Does he know the code? Surely not. Can the wooden staff prior open the safe door or knock the handle off? Doubtful. So, what he was going to do, we won't know. At the time he was trying to figure it out, the cleaning crew arrived. They saw him, screamed and ran away and he followed suit. He escaped and hid in the woods. The cleaning crew's arrival was his only saving grace for why he didn't trip any alarms and get caught. I'm not sure if the place had working cameras but no one ever found him hiding out in the woods. Shortly after that, probably because he was still hungry, he rejoined normal society and found himself living in a house versus in the woods and buying food instead of trying to rob a place in order to eat. He did eventually thrive while living in California. He found work as an extra in popular television shows and found himself a Fijian sugar momma (an older, wealthy woman for those of you who needed an explanation for that term).

Eventually he joined the Marines (a HUGE thank you to him and all of those who have served in the military for our country). When he was going through the process of enlisting, they, of course, did a background check and all their official things they must go through to make sure someone is suitable for this path. In doing so they found that he had a fine of approximately six grand from driving with an expired license plate. What probably would have been a $50 fine, turned into about $6,000. He, once again, just had the mindset that if he ignores it, it'll go away. Hopefully he learned that lesson but then again, now, he doesn't have a car to worry about that so that's good. More on his current life later.

Back to his time spent in the military. He did tours in Afghanistan and Iraq during what can understatedly be called a tumultuous time to be serving there. Not that those places are usually high on the hotspot list of places for Americans to vacation but during the early 2000s, for those of you who can remember, we were in the middle of a war on terrorism. While he was in the Marines during active duty though wasn't the only time he ever got shot at.

Let's chat for a minute about a quick trip that he and Ron took to Montgomery, Alabama to visit an Army Ranger friend who was stationed there. As they tell it, it started off as one of the greatest nights ever. They were bar hopping and having a good time. At one bar, when Sonny went to the bathroom, the boys told the bartender that they were going to order shots but to put water in theirs and actual vodka in Sonny's. After many rounds of these drinks, you can imagine the shape Sonny was in. They decide to end the night where many of us have, at Waffle House, and formulate a plan to try to get back home. Of course, it was very late, and this was before Uber or Lyft, and taxi service was scarce. A couple guys next to them eating overhear their conversation and offer to give them a ride if they pitch in for gas. Happy to give them some money in exchange for a lift, they get in the car. Now, as I mentioned, their group consisted of a Marine, and Army Ranger, and another athletically built guy so you can imagine that the three of them are not small dudes people could easily push around and as men, I'm sure they didn't think that much could or would happen to them.

As a woman, I would never get into the car with one random guy let alone multiple ones, unless my location can be tracked via a car service app, but that's neither here nor there.

Well, they're in the car and the driver decides they need to make a stop. In the projects. Now Sonny may not be too street smart but Ron certainly is, or claims to be. At this point he knows that "making a stop" either means they're getting drugs or shit is about to go down for them. The driver and other passenger get out and next thing you know Ron's door opens and he feels cold steel against his head. Let me mention that Sonny is passed out in the back of the car and so is their friend (he may not have taken as many shots as Sonny, but the alcohol clearly snuck up on him).

Then a person with a sawed-off shotgun steps in front of the car. They shake the passed-out guys awake to request all their money and for them to empty their pockets. Now part of me is surprised Sonny didn't try to talk to them and change the situation but of course, he was not in his normal state of mind. After that, luckily, they decide to let them go but as they are running away, they shoot at them. This was probably just to scare them but I'm sure it worked. Little did anyone know at that moment, an off-duty police officer was sitting nearby and he called the gunshot noise in and on-duty police officers came rushing to the scene. They came almost immediately, thinking the shots were directed at their fellow officer but then after finding my brothers and their friend they learned the entire story and the officers caught the guys soon after that.

At some point when Sonny was between jobs, I can vividly remember seeing him sport these new crocodile skin shoes. I'm not sure if they were real or fake crocodile skin, I didn't bother asking. I'm not sure where he got them, I didn't bother asking. I'm not sure how much they cost, I didn't bother asking. All I could think of was that Big Tymers rap song, "Still Fly". "Gator boots with the pimped out Gucci suits. Ain't got no job, but I stay sharp. Can't pay my rent, 'cause all my money's spent. But that's okay, 'cause I'm still fly."

He'd come around the corner poking his head and foot out and ask, "Have you seen my gatas??" His gatas, oh my word. And that's Sonny. And you just have to laugh. And now, if you're anything like me, you'll have that song stuck in your head for a solid 48 hours.

One summer afternoon I walked into the backyard of our

grandma's house. While I expected for both my brothers to be swimming in the pool, who I found surprised me. I see this guy with braids who has his entire body hair bleached blonde. As I get closer, I see that this isn't a stranger taking a dip and trying to cool off. This head-to-toe blondie was Sonny. He naturally has dark hair so needless to say this was quite the shock. But that's him and if he's going to do something, it's going to be all the way. He then asked me to grab the stopwatch he had at the side of the pool and time him while he dove underwater. He was attempting to break the world record for the longest amount of time anyone has held their breath underwater. And dammit, he actually did get pretty close to the current record. Sadly, he never got to claim the title though.

After a handful of years in the military and seeing things that I don't want to imagine, Sonny left the Marines and decided a life off the grid would, once again, be a better choice. So back to Fiji he went. He wanted to farm and live off the land, though he knew very little about either of those things. Despite that, I applaud wanting to rediscover yourself and reconnect with your roots.

During his time back in Fiji he met his wife and they now have four kiddos. In the course of the time when only two of their kids had been born, Sonny went through a born-again Christian phase. Born-again Christian is wonderful. Any type of newfound faith can be beautiful.

I am a faith-based woman and follower of Christ,

however, because there is no in between with him and he's either all in or all out, he took it to an extreme place. He got swept away. Went a bit off the deep end. Very Old Testament if you will. Fire and brimstone. He didn't want his kids believing in Santa. Nope, shut that down really quick. I get it. Jesus is the reason for the season and all of that, but Santa is just plain fun if he doesn't overshadow the real meaning of Christmas.

He also got into some conspiracy theories about this, that, and the other. Now listen, after being in the military and seeing some stuff, heck, without being in the military and seeing some stuff, I understand how you question things. And I, too, have gone down many a rabbit hole of conspiracy theories about our country, God, etc., but diving too deep and getting too consumed with those things can become a slippery slope into living alone in a basement somewhere, writing on the walls, and never turning on any lights. Sometimes you just have to force yourself to not get too wrapped up and see the silver lining and maybe even drink a little bit of the ignorance-is-bliss Kool-Aid when it comes to that. Anyway, I am happy to report that he didn't spend too much time in conspiracy and over-the-top extremist land. All is well and Santa is a thing.

Because living off the land is very difficult and has more challenges than sometimes expected, Sonny has worked a variety of jobs on their small island in Fiji to help support his family.

One of my favorite jobs he's had was working as a driver for the show Survivor. Now, I never got into this show but I remember one of my college roommates being obsessed with it and clearly loads of people feel the same because there have been 40 seasons of the program. The show places a group of strangers in remote lands and sees which one can survive the longest. They form alliances and vote people off and whoever is the last one standing, wins what I'm assuming is a pile of money and of course the notoriety and pride that comes along with being named the ultimate survivor. Again, I've never watched it so my apologies if I didn't adequately explain the viewing program well enough for the Survivor enthusiasts out there.

Back to Sonny. It was a great gig that he had as a driver for the show's production team and all of those who weren't actively in survival mode, but the irony is that he should be the one staring on the show. Between his time as an extra actor in Hollywood and the fact that he survives remote island life daily, it always seemed more suiting to me that he should've starred versus simply worked behind the scenes. Lord knows he would make an excellent character.

To add one more random fact for Sonny, because as if he wasn't difficult enough to try to pinpoint and visualize, he is an incredibly talented artist. He can draw. I remember him creating these etched pieces of artwork on black paper that were fascinating and neat. I always am blown away by artists because I very much lack any artistic ability. Can I be creative in other ways? Sure, but I don't even excel in stick figure art. Our mom, as moms do, has kept artwork my brothers and I have done over the years and it's just embarrassing. She would hate to know that I've thrown some away when she wasn't looking. Mom, you can keep Sonny's stuff but not my square-shaped fish project that I clearly should have failed.

Sonny still lives in Fiji, in the village he was born in, with his adorable family. He has painted their home with various Bible verses and abstract artwork. If you're ever interested in visiting, I'm sure he'd be happy to host you.

You may have been wondering, as you read about Sonny, as I would have been as well, if he ever went to jail. No, no he didn't. At least not up until the time this book has been released and I pray I never have to revise that statement.

LESSONS LEARNED:

- Give zero effs. Not in an unruly or rude way but rather as a way of not caring what others have to think and listening to your own inner guide. Don't care what the perceived accepted or expected thing is; do what your heart says. And when you make up your mind, don't let others persuade you. You can take their advice, hear them out, but trust yourself.
- Be honest.

CHAPTER FIVE

KNUCKLEHEAD UNCLE

Uncle David. Grandpa Dave Dog. Effing David.

I honestly don't know any other way to start his chapter but like that. Claiming all his titles for one to pick from. He can be a total shit. My earliest memories of him include him calling me shit-for-brains and me bawling because I was so upset.

Now that I'm older, I understand him, and I can hold my own better by just dishing it back. And buying him fake medication pills for anti-bullshit. He used to pretend to forget, or maybe he really didn't remember, what the term is for someone who doesn't consume animal products, but he would always ask if I was still a vixen. Yes, David, I am still a vegan. That one would make me laugh. I do think his mocking or a-hole tendencies can sometimes be seen as endearing but sometimes it would come off as just plain mean.

You've just gotta learn to sort through what is what with him. And then, know when and how to react and dish it back. We all have folks in our lives like this. But anyway, he's that guy. He will continue to give people crap, ragging on anyone and everyone.

To further visualize David, picture David Spade minus any

hair on his face or on his head. He's the guy who wears graphic tees that say things like "Beer, bacon, and bass fishing" or "If you don't like this country then you can leave." You know the type; I know you do. When you're around him, the time is mostly spent either rolling your eyes or laughing at him and dismissing his ridiculousness. Sometimes, though, time is spent crying as a handful of family members have experienced. But the funny, or interesting thing rather, is that he's fairly sensitive himself. Thus, one could deduct that dishing BS out to others is his way of deflecting his own personal vulnerabilities, but we won't get into a psychoanalysis of him.

He's a classic guy. He listens to late 1970s and early 1980s rock as well as country with some of his favorite bands and musicians being Queen and Tom Petty (if we could please have another moment of silence for his passing because I'm still not over it). I always feel like people's music choices can tell a lot about someone. Glance at a mixtape they've made or a playlist they've compiled and it's as though you're peering into their soul. It's intimate and revealing.

My musical choices range from Nine Inch Nails to Lauren Daigle to country to absolutely some old school rap. It's all over the place. It's sometimes a scary place to be, experiencing someone you thought you knew and their musical tastes, so tread lightly. But other times, it's exactly what you expect, like with David. No curveballs there.

In recent years, on a trip down to Florida to visit family, including me and my husband, he created the Take Your Uncle Drinking Day or TYUDD as we now refer to it. This day has now turned into an annual event, occurring on the last weekend in April, barring a global pandemic or freak phenomena. Your official TYUDD day can fall on any day of that weekend. It consists of an uncle and niece or nephew combination and all day eating and drinking around your designated area of bars and restaurants. The niece or nephew oversees hosting and making the list of places to go and the uncle goes where he's told. Yes, it's fun bonding but one of the best parts? The uncle is in charge of paying for everything. Score!

David is a social butterfly so I think his creation of TYUDD was his way of getting out of the condo and exploring the local scene more. Much like Anna with Ron, my aunt shakes her head when he's striking up a conversation with strangers around him. He probably should have been in sales, advertising, or marketing because he'd make sure all of those near us knew exactly what we were out on the town for and convince them they needed to join in the TYUDD festivities.

The most recent TYUDD Jeff's uncle joined us as well as my stepdad's nephew. Each year our group is growing, and it's hysterical. Uncle David even insisted we have a Facebook page for it so check it out and bring it to a city near you.

Now let's bring it back to David's earlier days.

As the second youngest of five kids, David was your classic middle child. Do a quick internet search for middle child syndrome and there you will find a lot of his traits. He loved being the center of attention yet would play the woe-is-me card (he may still have a little bit of this in him now). But he was an adorable little boy. Think Ralphie from the movie a *Christmas Story* except without glasses. Goofy little kid with a cheesy grin. But as innocent as he may have looked, as he got to be a little bit older, he turned into a bit of a kleptomaniac. He would steal records or food with really no other reason but to do it. Probably seeking the thrill to escape the small-town monotony.

The North Dakota small town he and his siblings grew up in is the stereotypical small farming town. The town that country artists write songs about. You'll exit the interstate and drive down a long road with fields on both sides simply to enter the town. From there you can branch off the main drag and hop on any number of dirt roads. There are a handful of traffic lights, handful of restaurants, one major grocery store and fewer and fewer mom and pop shops. It had a drive-in theatre back in the day. The smell of the town is something unique to anywhere I've traveled. I've tried to pinpoint that smell every time I've been there, but I can never settle on what it is. Bread being toasted is the closest description I can get. I think the aroma must be from the large sugar beet plant in town and the locals are pretty much immune to it. The smell of sugar beets and boredom.

One of David's friend's parents owned a grocery story. David and his friend were going camping but instead of asking his friend's parents if they could have or work for some steaks to grill, he just decided to pick up some on his own with that five-finger discount.

My favorite klepto story is when he would steal records. Living and growing up in North Dakota it gets cold. Colder than you could imagine. Negative temps that will freeze your eyelids shut if you stay out too long, type of cold. So, needless to say, he had plenty of long, heavy winter jackets. The one he liked best for his life of crime was a long down coat with large pockets. He and his friends would go scope out the latest selection of tunes and he would somehow sneakily add them to his deep pockets. They never got caught and he only recently told his mom, Grandma Pat, about these wild adventures. Ah, back in my day we could steal music easily simply by using Napster.

He also would steal beer from random garages when he was underage and his stockpile was low. I do believe they were his friends or their parents' houses at least. Actually, I think it was the same family who owned the grocery store. Oh, how I love the stories you find out about as you get older about the elders in your family.

At our family cabins, he'll get up at 8 a.m. to start yard work and then be pissed when everyone else doesn't follow suit. Or actually, he will just operate power tools and lawnmowers outside your window so you don't have a choice but to wake up.

Speaking of cabins, over the last handful of years we all have decided to work on our family's cabins to fix them up. Well, that has been a constant process, but we decided to get serious with it as of late. So instead of doing some good ole fashioned DIY and renovation projects, he decided to simply have their existing cabin removed and just bring in a new two-story modular home. That's one way to quickly check off your honey-do list.

David always wants to be in charge and there is most certainly nothing passive about him. And he's stubborn. He is getting slightly better the older he gets and we are all very glad it's not the opposite, although I don't know how much more headstrong one could get. Maybe it's the grandbabies he has and adores. That has probably softened his edge a bit. He always thinks he knows best. And there's no convincing him otherwise. This has made him an expert in his professional life selling insurance, at which he's been very successful.

But he hasn't quite realized, or admitted at least, that he isn't an expert at everything. I won't give you a knock-down-drag-out fight of a debate example but here's a mild one.

David, always tinkering to improve something at home or the cabins, had a plethora of weeds he needed to get rid of to improve landscaping around his cabin. He decided on what to use and he attempted to go to work. Let me pause here and say that the cabin next to his family's is shared by my cousins who are brother and sister. Well one of them happens to be a landscape architect. This is his chosen career path and a passion he has had for many, many years. He is also an organic farmer. He knows a thing or two about a thing or two. To me, it would seem reasonable that if one were going to make some landscaping changes or possibly some adjustments, he would be a great person to chat with. An expert, if you will. See if maybe he had any advice or feedback.

But does David do this? Of course not. He doesn't need any stinkin' help. Well almost instantaneously as Dave is heading out to work on his yard, my cousin sees him and bombards him with questions, feedback, and his personal and professional opinions. After all, what David would be using is his soil, impacts the soil of those around him. He's not thinking like this though. David's not so much for science sometimes or even basic logic. He's for what really works and if it ain't broke then he's not trying to fix it. I think after my cousin pleaded his case and offered him a plethora of alternatives to what he wanted to use, and remind him that he probably didn't want his grandbabies playing is poison, David huffed and puffed away and gave in. To you, this may not sound like a win, but the fact that he backed down at all is a big deal. This means he was listening and either somewhat agreed or just didn't want to argue anymore. Both are huge wins.

Give him a few G&Ts (that's Gin and Tonics if you're a

more wholesome non-drinker or if you simply don't know the shortened term) and he will ghost out from a party. Or give an Irish goodbye. Or any other terms I may not know about which mean to leave a gathering without telling anyone. Simply disappear. Most likely to go to bed by his 8 p.m. bedtime. That, of course, is only after he has talked loudly and obnoxiously about political views or other hot topic items that certainly pissed some people off. In the morning, you (usually) can't help but love him again. Especially after he gives you the Silewski Scrunch Face.

They say everyone has a serial killer trait. Something that if that person ever became a serial killer, we'd look back and say, because of blank, we should have known. Something along the lines of people who sleep in their socks or people who pour milk into their bowl before cereal.

Think about it.

Let me give you another few examples. Jeff has a friend who has two traits that would absolutely be his signs and these things go together. Let me explain, he is practically obsessive compulsive with his cleaning and general Type A personality. For example, if you're making a peanut butter and jelly sandwich at their house you can't use the same knife to get the peanut butter and then dip it into the jelly. Absolutely not. You get a clean knife. Okay, I get that. I don't do that at my own home (a little PB in my J is okay with me) but that's fine. So, he does that but then here's the kicker, the dude bites his toenails instead of trimming them with clippers. Like, seriously, WTF? What in the actual eff?! I will never, for as long as I live, understand this.

Now back to David. His serial killer trait, if I had to pick one, would likely be that he wears his socks halfway on his feet when he's inside the house. I don't know how to comprehend this. For one, I have a thing with socks. I am anal retentive when it comes to the seams. If any bit of the seam is too much on the side or underneath my foot, I can't handle it. I worry that my daughter is inheriting this too because she spazzed out the other day when I was helping her put on her socks. I need to know if this is a trait that can be passed down to next generations! And if so, what can I do to stop it? But it may be too late.

The only reason I say this is likely David's serial killer trait, not positively or certainly, is because this trait, interestingly enough, is also a trait of a few of my cousins. And these cousins of mine are not his children, mind you. Like, what the heck? I don't understand this. Is only the front part of your foot cold? Does your heel get excessively warm? Again, other things I need to know! I will know that if they all end up becoming serial killers this is, absolutely, 100%, the trait we will trace it back to. Take note that these may be warning signs. I don't like it. I'm not comfortable with this whatsoever.

All of this aside, he is generous, very nice, and exceptionally fun. And he has some of the whitest teeth I have ever seen. His kids make fun of his Chicklets, but I applaud the guy. I, too, appreciate snow white teeth and bleaching mine but he certainly gives me and anyone I know a run for our money. I believe his kids are genuinely worried his teeth are going to fall out one day because of this.

He has helped many people in our family out when they've been in financial trouble and will help his neighbors with chores as if they are his own. Although don't you dare try to get him to do your cabin chores; that's where he draws the line.

He went on a mission trip to Africa with his local church a few years ago. It changed his life. This was the first time David went out of the country minus to Canada or Mexico. He was generous before but that will, or should, make anyone rethink and reevaluate how we look at our own lives.

Uncle David talks or texts his two kids every day. Every. Single. Day. I honestly don't know many parents who do this. He is very much a family man. He's the dad who was always there for his children's games or events. He is the grandpa who will take time off work to go see his granddaughter at school or bring her class treats. The one who will take all his grandchildren hunting or boating or whatever activity they want to do. So, while he can often be strong-willed and sometimes confrontational, he's also a sweet guy. He truly is. He was a momma's boy and very protective of my Grandma Pat. I'm not talking about a codependent relationship, still living in his mom's basement, or any negative connotation in regards to the term momma's boy. Merely, the baby boy of his family loving his momma dearly. There's something to be said for men who help care for their moms.

He's also silly and fun and kind.

If you ever want to experience this man, check out the TYUDD Facebook page, find where we will be during our next annual event, grab your uncle, and join us.

LESSONS LEARNED:

- Hold family close to your heart and fight for them.
- Embrace people's differences, even when you strongly disagree with them.
- Get out of your comfort zone. It will be life-changing. Whether it's for God or for another cause you believe in or just for self-growth, do it. Force yourself to do things you either couldn't ever imagine doing or things that scare you. Those things are the things that will change you. Make you grow. Evolve. Make you a better person. For me personally, those things often come from traveling. I believe there is nothing like traveling when it comes to self-exploration and growth. When you are not in your familiar surroundings and you are immersed in a culture different than your own, you learn about yourself. Some of the things you'll learn you won't like and some you will but either way you are learning and discovering new parts of yourself and you'll be better for

it. And if you're looking for a sign to do that thing you've been debating but your soul keeps nudging you to do, take this as it. This is your sign.
- Have your uncle take you out and pay for everything.

CHAPTER SIX

COUSIN FULL OF CONTRADICTIONS

Back to the topic of giving zero effs. Meet my cousin Miranda.

While she is laid-back and chill and yet uber outgoing, she, similar to Sonny, is unpredictable. She has no shame. Book smart yet spacey. Again, much like my oldest brother.

She's the girl who loses her driver's license but is able to get onto a plane with a Costco card. The woman who served our country in the Air Force and knows how to speak Arabic. She's hard to decipher. If you saw her, without hearing anything come out of her mouth, you may assume she's prime and proper. She looks cute and innocent, but she's got almost a half-sleeve of tattoos and a mouth that's going to tell anyone how and what she thinks. She is one of the most hysterical people I know. She is that person that can make any situation into a story. In fact, we've told her for many years she needs to write a book because, for one, we want to read it and, two, anyone would find it funny. But until she does, my own recapping of her stories will have to do.

Let me start with the Costco card story. My cousins and I are all very close. We have a blast together. Most of us are married with kids and we've decided that time just us, just the OG cousins (plus the "outlaws" as we lovingly refer to those who married into our incredible family), is a necessity. Plus, we are now old enough to afford going away on trips.

With that, we have begun an annual cousin trip. We pick places that are easy for all of us to get to, as we live in a variety of places across the United States. Places that people haven't been before or places that are just fun. Our first annual trip was to Nashville. In what I will tell you is typical Miranda fashion, she confused both the dates and times of everyone's arrival and departure. She confused the day everyone arrived, thinking we are all there a day before her, and then confused the day everyone left, leaving later than everyone else.

But this is just the beginning. You know during the trip there will be stories of her. She has a fancy camera that she brought on the trip to document the shenanigans, rather than taking phone photos, which I can fully appreciate. Throughout the trip people assumed she was either our hired photographer or paparazzi, which I guess would have meant the rest of us are some sort of important people needing to get our pictures taken. Then again, everyone in Nashville is trying to be somebody so this does all make sense. She, of course, plays into this. But the real funny parts with her come when we all must leave. Most of us flew out early so we could get home at decent times. Miranda scheduled her flight for later but since we were all going to be gone (recall her timing confusion mentioned above), she figured she'd ride to the airport with us to try to catch an earlier flight. With no luck in accomplishing this, she heads back into the city for a solo adventure. During this time, she gets food, is mistaken for a bum (no idea how or why), goes ice skating (because, why not?), and loses her ID somewhere. When it's finally her time to head home, she arrives at the airport and cries to airport security, begging them to let her on the plane even though her ID is MIA.

Someway, somehow, this works, and they let her on the plane using her Costco card. I mean, it does have your picture on it, so it seems somewhat legit, right? Probably the fact she was in the military helped. I'm okay with that to be honest. Those who serve our country deserve special treatment.

Shenanigans. That's a perfect word for her. She gets into shenanigans no matter where she goes. She just can't help herself.

She will randomly say things either aloud in a group setting or on her social media to no one in particular like, "I wish you could boost your credit score by doing side quests. Like, I'm not great at managing debt but I fought a troll under a bridge. Can I buy a house now? Wishful thinking. But I couldn't fight a troll anyway, so I don't know why I'm concerned with this hypothetical." Excuse me, what?!

This is how her brain works. 24/7. I can be random, but she takes it to a new level. And then makes it humorous. I bet she laughs at herself when she's home alone. Just giggles thinking about things and, most likely, saying them aloud.

She's a tough chick. And I don't only say this because she grew up playing hockey. Although I love that about her. I can't imagine myself playing hockey. Now, granted, I didn't grow up in Minnesota where it's an incredibly popular sport, but still. I think even if I had it wouldn't have been my thing. I love watching it and especially love being at games, but I'll leave the actual playing for others.

When I say she's tough I not only mean physically, and this little broad is a petite thing so don't get the wrong image in your head, I also mean emotionally. Her first marriage was filled mostly with turmoil and that's putting it lightly. She got out of an abusive relationship and the nasty divorce that came with it, graduated from the Air Force Academy, raised her daughter alone, and pushed through it better than most people I know would have.

She overcame and is a total badass. She got remarried to a lovely man who's taken her little girl as his own and they now have two other kiddos together. These two are great together. He mellows her out and is the yin to her yang or whatever the kids are saying these days (I don't think it's actually that, by the way).

Also, she can play the violin and the banjo, both badass instruments in my book and reflective of her polarizing personality traits.

Back to her having no shame. She once pooped on the side of the road while staring at her now husband. Mostly to prove a point, I think. She had to go and I think there was a disagreement about when the next stop would be and therefore in the middle of a California traffic jam, she exited the car and let loose. Another cousin of mine said that somehow, Miranda finds herself pooping her pants often, but I've never been privy enough to witness it (not sure if this is fortunate or unfortunate for me). Since I haven't, I'll give her the benefit of the doubt because as an adult, I'm not sure how it would happen that she would find herself in such sticky (no pun intended) situations. Barf.

Surprisingly I have a similar story about one of my best girlfriends pooping her pants. But she was a kid. In elementary school. Still rather old to not be able to hold it but makes more sense than being a full-blown adult. So, she was in elementary school and she and her brother were heading home from the bus stop and she had to go. Badly. She asked her brother to hold her rolling (or rollie as she called it) backpack while she hurried inside but it was too late. Her bowels let loose all over her beloved rollie backpack. None of us can ever look at those bags the same ever again.

Miranda loves her kids and is a great mom. But she has no shame in poking fun at them and sharing nontraditional parenting hacks. I always appreciate parents who are like this. Our world, at least I feel this way especially for women and moms, is so consumed with being the best. Being superior to others. Having it more together than the next person. Very edited and seemingly fake. Only showing the highlight reels, although I am probably guilty of sometimes wanting to do that as well. Damn our society!

It's hard to show people the shitty things that are going wrong but the more we do, the more others can relate. More people have hiccups in their days than have perfect days (whatever that means), especially when it comes to kids.

The latest parenting hack Miranda has begun sharing relates to eyebrows. Let me give a little background. We are cousins because my mom and her dad are siblings. Their mother is Grandma Pat. As I mentioned, Pat's last name is Silewski. The Silewski name is Polish. Our family has a lot of little blue-eyed, blonde-haired members. Miranda did not inherit any such Slavic characteristics, as she very much favors her mother who possesses Native Americans roots (roots in which she cherishes and honors very much). Her son, however, is a little blondie, which coincidentally means he has extremely light eyebrows. Actually, his eyebrows are almost nonexistent. A fact he is aware of and concerned with. I, too, feel his pain as I was passed down this genetic sadness as well.

Now back to Miranda's parenting hack.

Her son was resisting eating his dinner. Thinking quickly, Miranda told him that the reason he has no eyebrows is because kids only get them from eating fruits and vegetables. Her son was immediately concerned and shaped up then and there, piling food into his mouth. She's not sure how long he will believe this and she's aware he may need therapy when he gets older but feels happy that her child won't get scurvy. And let's be real, we all need therapy anyway, so we might as well be healthy going into it. And again, as someone whose eyebrows are practically nonexistent and needs to pencil them in on the daily, I respected this trick of hers. Although, I wish it were true because if it were, my eyebrows would be banging with my plant-based diet.

Even if she wasn't my cousin, she would still be one of my favorite people to follow on social media. She posts the funniest things, whether it's random memes she makes or finds somewhere in the depths of the internet, or things her kids do or just her thoughts.

For example, while she was pregnant with her third baby, she had a craving for mashed potatoes. I can totally relate to that. If you've either ever been pregnant or been around a woman who is pregnant and experiencing cravings, you know how strong those cravings are. You will move mountains to get her what she's asking for.

Her husband, excitedly, thinks he's doing her a favor and brings her back cauliflower mashed potatoes. She, of course, has a fit. "Don't tell me that cauliflower is a potato substitute. I will lose all trust in your taste buds. I don't care. Gordon Ramsey could say that to me and I could slap him right in the nose!" Don't mess with cravings. Don't substitute anything a pregnant lady is asking for. Ever.

These are the types of things she makes funny. Normal, everyday occurrences that most people would barely even think twice about.

I also need to give her husband some credit. He is one of the nicest, kindest people I've met and he would move Earth to make her and their kids happy. So, his enthusiasm over what he thought would be a hit, was just another gesture of him being sweet.

But again, I repeat, don't mess with pregnancy cravings. Don't alter them and damn sure don't try to switch it for something you think would be better either taste or health wise.

Another day in the life moment of Miranda's she shared via video. On this video she's running her fingers through her hair and whipping it back and forth as if she's Willow Smith. She then says, "Totally unnecessary for me to flex on y'all like this, it's just that I'm about to go to bed and my hair looks amazing. It's just a good hair evening. Goodnight and I hope the Boogeyman is ready for these glossy strands." She is not full of herself or overly involved in her looks so that's where the humor really comes into play. But you know what? We should all be happy to share when we look damn good. Even if it is before hopping into bed. And we should be happy to see when others look their best too. And this is coming from me, the woman who has been cutting her own hair, uses loads of dry shampoo, and rarely styles it so I'm definitely not simply looking for an excuse to toot my own horn.

Her kids are quickly becoming as funny as she is. When her daughter was younger, Miranda spoke to her only in Arabic and then she went to a Spanish immersion daycare. I, as I'm certain Miranda did, would have thought this was a wonderful idea. Surely, this will help her daughter be so advanced and so far ahead of kids her age. Kids are sponges and they take to, learn, and remember languages very well.

Unfortunately, it didn't turn out that way.

Not a shock for anyone who has kids. We all know that the picture in our heads is not often the reality we find ourselves in. Her daughter now only seems to remember random curse words in Arabic and random food words in Spanish. She'll ask Miranda things such as, "Mommy, what does alqarf mean?" It means shit. Miranda will then have to tell her it's a bad word or explain it to her in a way only she would. My personal favorite way to explain cursing to children is to say that those are adult words. Words you can decide to say or not when you're older. That way you're not constantly getting shamed by children for saying bad words. Not that I make it a habit to cuss often in front of kids. Or her daughter will say something along the lines of talking about quesadillas and think she's fluent in español.

Two of Miranda's kids now want their own YouTube channels and I think she should allow it. They want to talk about toys or do shows or whatever it is little minds think is important. I bet people would watch it! Some kids are making millions off doing random crap on there like that, so hey, why not? I encourage and support it. YouTubing your kids out or putting them on social media in an attempt to gain notoriety is this generation's pageant mom.

Miranda, keep being random, girl. Keep being you. We need more people like you in our world.

LESSONS LEARNED:

- Be a tough chick. Or if you're a guy, just be tough. I don't mean macho; I simply mean stand your ground. Get out of situations you don't need to be in.
- See the humor in everything.
- Tell it like it is and have no shame. Stop waiting for permission to be who you want; to be who you are. Don't be scared to share when things aren't perfect.
- Be laidback. I'm especially speaking to myself with this one. Sometimes we all need to take a chill pill.
- As Miranda does with appreciating and advocating for her Native American culture with her kids and family, be true to your roots and embrace your heritage.

CHAPTER SEVEN
GRACIOUS GRANNY

My Grandma Reid is one of the nicest people I know and I'm not just saying this because I'm pretty sure I'm her favorite, which, if I am, I have no idea why or what I did to deserve that, but I will take it.

Anyway, it's not only me who she's nice to. She adores all her grandkids and kids and is so sweet to my grandpa. Now granted, my grandpa takes excellent care of her and is such a gem himself. They have what I think is an adorable relationship. They both take good care of each other. She is the person who you want to talk to when you're feeling down or being hard on yourself as she will compliment you left and right until suddenly, you're feeling better about yourself.

Now that we're all getting older, the responsibility to call and check in falls more on me so I have a reminder in my calendar to call every so often. I despise talking on the phone. I usually prefer texting over any other form of communication. With my grandparents there's an exception though. This doesn't apply to them. I know these calls will be short and sweet both literally and figuratively.

The phone conversation goes like this: I call, they answer, they express how wonderful it is to hear from me, my grandmother says how beautiful my family is and how special we all are and how proud they are and they always end the call by saying how much they love me. It's precious and I cherish those moments and will miss them when they are gone. But my favorite conversations of all with them are when they call me on my birthday. Regardless if I answer or if they leave a voicemail, they always sing "Happy Birthday" (and again say how lovely I am and how proud they are). One year I intentionally didn't answer because I wanted to have a voice message from them that I could keep forever.

My birthday is important to me. I am the person who observes the holiday all month long and who believes every trip around the sun is a reason to celebrate. Grandma Reid is the same way. She would throw super special parties for my grandpa and always decorate their condo with loads of signs and pictures and gifts. She'd write birthday cards using precious bubble letters and decorate them with printed pictures. The cards would include verbiage such as "The best person in the world is having a birthday and you deserve the best always" and "Wishing you good luck and good health and a happy heart always." She'd even decorate wrapping paper and their mirrors around their condo with these sweet notes and heart and star drawings. It's simply adorable. It really is the little things, isn't it?

Along the lines of birthdays and little things. My grandma never could remember to take the price tag off any of her gifts. It became a standing joke in my family. Whenever one of us would open a gift from her, we'd just look at one another and chuckle under our breath and we all knew what the joke was. I'd say we aren't laughing at her but rather laughing with her but I'm pretty sure none of us ever told her she always left them on. I still wouldn't say we were laughing at her though.

So, usually, a divorce is not a good thing. Well, really it never is. But to look on the bright side, and a bit selfish side, the fact that my dad's parents got divorced simply means I got more grandparents to love and love on me. My Grandma Reid is my dad's stepmom. For grandkids, and again, I know this is being selfish, it works out pretty well and my kids can now benefit from the same thing since my folks got divorced and both are remarried. Trying to focus on the silver lining here, you know?

Even with the separations and remarriages, I am saddened to think I only have one set of grandparents still around, not counting step-grandparents or grandparents by marriage. And honestly, the rawness and realness of speaking this aloud puts me in shock. Even if I do count the step-grands and grandparents on Jeff's side of the family, we have barely a handful still with us. Going from having a plethora of them, to now so few, I want to cherish them more. Of course, I should have been doing this all along but somewhere in our minds I think we assume our grandparents will always be around. They always have been, our entire lives, so why would that change? I understand the absurdness and unrealistic nature of this, but I believe many of us think like this.

I had grandparents pass away when I was younger but at those times, I didn't grasp it as much as I do now. I've had grandparents suddenly taken from this world and so there isn't much to do but mourn. There was nothing to have been done differently, although you could say, of course, that every day is a gift and nothing is promised and to never take anyone or anything for granted or YOLO (you only live once) as the kids are saying these days. Often that's easier said than done. We can have that mindset for a short bit of time and then we get back to our daily lives so that sentiment sort of wears off if we aren't careful.

In this situation with my Grandma Reid, and even my Grandpa Reid, now that I can vividly see before my eyes the decline in health, I want to make sure I am being mindful in my relationship with them and doing what I can to cherish the remaining time. We never want to look back and wish we had done more. This is the only benefit to a slow fade because the rest of it involved with watching anyone or anything decline is damn hard. This makes me think of one of my favorite songs. Well, it was actually a speech for a late 1990s graduation ceremony that a filmmaker by the name of Baz Luhrman recited. It's called "Everybody's Free (To Wear Sunscreen)". It talks about, as you would have maybe guessed, wearing sunscreen and the importance in that, but it also talks about enjoying your youth and your body. Appreciate how fabulous you look and to use your body in every way you can, not being ashamed or afraid of it or worried about what others will think. He's right when he says it's the greatest instrument we will ever own. We can't take it for granted. He also reminds us that we are not as fat as we imagine. Can I get an amen? Hallelujah!

Why are grandparents, usually mostly grandmas, usually so good at showing people how much they mean to them? They pinch your cheeks (usually really freakin' hard) and give you big hugs and just love all over you. Grandma Reid does just that. She is extremely proud of her family and they, and everyone else, know it. She isn't only proud in the way moms or grandmas usually are but in a truly glowing when she talks about people, type of way. And dammit, we all need someone to feel like that about us, for us. Someone who boosts our confidence. Someone who makes us simply feel better than okay about ourselves.

Is gambling a trait most grandmas have in common or only mine? Grandma Reid takes after my Grandma Pat and loves to get her gamble on. She favors the slot machines mostly. Nothing crazy. Nothing expensive. Just silly fun slots. Going to a casino with her is something I've never experienced but maybe I should add that to my bucket list.

In what I think is true grandparent form, one of her favorite restaurants is the Macaroni Grill. My grandma is Lebanese and she loves traditional Lebanese cuisine (think tabbouleh, shawarma, falafel, hummus, baba ganoush, baklava, etc., as my mouth begins to water at the mere thought of these foods) so I'm not sure if this favorite is more so hers, or my grandpa's, or just a place she knows everyone can always find something they like. But regardless, every time we are in Detroit visiting them, we go there. I feel like this is a very grandma move. A very grandma place to go so while I'm very much down for local spots and exotic cuisines, I always smile and go willingly when she suggests we eat there.

Another random trait of my grandma is that she loves Louis Vuitton. She has purses, luggage, hanging garment covers, keychains, accessories -- you get the picture. Over the years as she goes out on the town less and stays at her home more, she has come to realize that I would appreciate these items and has given me a lot of her collection, which I absolutely value and cherish. I truly love any type of hand-me-down. I always have. Whether it's clothing from older cousins or jewelry from grandmas or items my mom has bought and realized she doesn't love, I honor and adore these items. As I've gotten older, I've realized that maybe all of these items aren't really LV, if you catch my drift, but they are really hers and that makes them invaluable. It's smart, giving your favorite people your favorite things that you don't use anymore, while you're still around to see them enjoy them. I can assure you, if you give someone something you love and the other person loves it too, they will appreciate them as much as you have and the joy it will bring to the other person is a gift in itself.

What's funny is that while she loves her some Louis, she also loves a good deal and loves to go garage sale-ing. This seems to be a recurring theme in my family even by those who aren't related to each other. Anyway, one time when we were visiting her, my brothers, my mom, my dad, and I filled up the entire back of our green Mercury minivan with garage sale finds. Seats down, loaded up with goods. Mostly for her. What everything was, I don't recall, but it was a lot of stuff.

Now for a slight detour from this story but on the topic of the van and a funny story nonetheless. My parents eventually sold that minivan but my mom left something inside of it. She was saddened by the thought she'd never see it again but eventually she forgot about it. That was until one day, my mom and I saw the minivan in the parking lot of a strip mall and decided to break in. Okay, they didn't change the code on the driver's side door so were we technically breaking in? I stood watch as she quickly entered and exited the car. We retrieved her item (why they still had it, I'm not sure) and couldn't contain the laughter for our close to criminal behavior.

I remember thinking that that van was the coolest. Now I want to stay as far away from minivans as I possibly can. No offense to anyone who has one; I understand the appeal. I just don't personally want to drive one. Ever. That van had controls in the backseat with a headphone plug in so the kids could listen to their own music and control things. It was unlike anything we ever had. Now, of course, vans like this are common for families with more than two kids and they've got TVs and vacuums and all sorts of shit built into them. But that Mercury was ahead of its time.

As you may assume by my grandma's love of luxury brands and products, she is a fashionable woman who likes to dress and look her best and who accessorizes with jewelry and brooches and, of course, a nice purse. Her and my Grandma Pierce (my dad's mom) had this in common. Ironically enough Grandma Pierce is Grandpa Reid's ex-wife who has now passed away so maybe he had somewhat of a type with his women. But their generation, as a whole, was slightly different than our generations as of late. Back then a woman wouldn't be caught dead going out of her house without lipstick. Some days I'm lucky I have a bra on to go out and about. Who am I kidding though? My boobies are way too relaxed to appear in public without one, if you're understanding what I'm saying. It would be fun to still dress up for every outing but it's also demanding and a lot of work.

Although Grandma Reid wants to present her best to the world and look well, she is not prideful and, for the most part, when it comes to mostly anything about her, she's modest. Besides her health, which she now often talks about, she really doesn't like to talk about herself. Honestly, she would probably not be thrilled anyone else was talking about her either, let alone writing about her to be captured forever. Sorry grandma, I love you!

LESSONS LEARNED:

- This is a tale as old as time (and if your brain works similarly to mine, you will now have that song from *Beauty and the Beast* on repeat in your head), but it probably cannot be stated enough: listen to your grandparents. If you're lucky enough to have your grandparents around into your adult life do what you can to learn from them. Hear what they have to say and truly listen. They have stories to tell and wisdom us younger folks can't even begin to understand but the more we hear, the better we will become. Usually, if you haven't heard the story 1,040,837 times, like often is the case with our grandparents, the stories will be entertaining or interesting or at least you'll learn something new about them. Or even better, you may learn something new, and if you're lucky, incriminating,

about your mom or dad.
- Tell people what you think of them and how you feel about them. Express how amazing you think they are. Give compliments out often. And on the flip side, when people express these things to you, believe them. Take the compliment. They mean it.
- Love your spouse or significant other greatly. The way she loves my grandpa (and the way he loves her too) is inspiring. You can see it in the way she looks at him and the way she tries to care for him and in the way she celebrates him and the things she says about him to others and to him. They put each other first without having other people feel left out. I don't feel like I'm this sweet to anyone but I'm trying because I'd dang sure like to be that way to my husband, at least, that's for sure.
- Keep phone calls short. Don't make people dread answering your calls. Make them enjoy answering and wait for the next time they happen with anticipation.
- Reminder that your kids or grandkids are never too old to want to hear you sing "Happy Birthday" to them. There is a sweet innocence about this that never seems to get old or go away.
- Give people your favorite things if you don't use them anymore, especially while you're still around. They will appreciate them as much as you have and then you will be able to see their joy with them.

CHAPTER EIGHT

UNCONVENTIONAL DAD

Me: "Okay, you'll pick me up from the airport?" Dad: "Yep, be there soon." Me: "Great, see you soon."

As soon as I land in Detroit, where we are meeting to visit the above-mentioned grandparents, in walks Robert, my dad, wearing the most mismatched outfit you've ever seen. Tribal button-down shirt with black and blue, probably from Fiji or Micronesia or another island country he lived and worked in, with flower shorts, probably the kind that zip off from pants.

I just look at him and shake my head, laugh, and quickly snap a picture with my phone. Luckily, I did not get my sense of fashion from him. I'm not pretending to be a fashionista. I often combine vintage with modern clothing and accessories and have a history of combing through the dELiA*s catalog. My style can be different but it's not Robert-level different.

But he doesn't care. He always tried to justify it and usually says that no one else will have it. That's his signature statement: "No one else will have it."

When he'd bring us things after returning from one of his trips, he'd say that. When it comes to souvenirs and memorabilia, that's a great perk. I have so many neat things from all over the world that he has brought me or sent me or gathered on my own during trips to see him.

Even when it comes to fashion, branching out and dressing like no one else can be a cool, trendy, hip thing but that's not the case with his style. I don't think he's trying to be on the cutting edge of fashion. Maybe it's a comfort thing. Maybe it's a never wanting to do laundry thing. I honestly don't know. But again, he doesn't care.

My brothers and I could poke fun or make all kinds of comments, but it wouldn't matter. It's never changed anything. Another classic outfit includes a button-down shirt with various shades of green blocks, some containing sea turtles, others with boats, others with plants paired with brown and blue plaid shorts. Always mixing patterns. I love a good pattern mixing but the trick is to make them look like they flow, not as though it's tacky dress up day in grade school. If we're being honest, it's become such a joke with us kids that if he stopped dressing that way, we probably wouldn't know how to handle it.

As I mentioned, he's lived and worked all over the world. His background is in international development. He's worked with the Peace Corps, Save the Children, the United States Embassy, and the United States Agency for International Development. Therefore, before he retired, he would need to dress up for work. He'd have meetings and work with people who are very high up in government agencies and other movers and shakers. Now, I'm sure at his important meetings he would look the part, but I can also imagine that for normal, everyday work his collection of wild ties would be in the daily mix. By now, I'm sure you can conjure up some thoughts of what those ties may look like and you'd probably be right.

All things considered, a plain Jane style simply wouldn't suit this man. Pleated khakis and an unadorned polo don't fit for someone who can speak a handful of languages, has lived all over the globe, and who has had more adventures in his life than most can imagine.

To end his style section and try to make sense of it, I think it's either that when you live at various places throughout the world you pick up different style trends and just combine them all together or it's that his style is to wear whatever the eff you want. You do you, dad.

One more thing regarding Robert's overall appearance, not simply his style choices. Along with saying that everyone has a serial killer trait (which, for my dad, I think we can chalk it up to his clothing choices because there may be a time we look back and reflect that we should've known given his unpredictable nature expressed via clothes), they also say that everyone has a doppelgänger. Doppelgänger is merely a fancy word for look-alike. Robert's doppelgänger is Kurt Rambis. Without older brothers, I would have never even known who Kurt Rambis was, let alone make a comparison of him favoring this man. If you have no idea who he is, I don't fault you. Kurt is a famous National Basketball Association player who spent most of his pro-baller time with the Los Angeles Lakers and then a handful more years as a coach, winning championships both as a player and as a coach. So, he's a pretty big deal. A popular guy. If you do a quick internet search with his name, chances are high that a picture of him playing basketball in his prime, during the early 1980s, will pop up. This picture will include his dark-rimmed glasses, fine, straight blonde hair, and a thick mustache. This, indeed, looks very much like my father has for a strong majority of my life. He's ditched the thick mustache as of late, but the other traits still favor ole Kurt.

The only look-alike my brothers have pointed out for me over the years (specifically circa early 1990s) is that I could be a missing Hanson brother. Their fourth bandmate. Thanks guys.

Now it seems like a total dad move to back into every car spot no matter where you're parking, how long you'll be there, etc. But is it also a total dad move to turn down the radio while you're finding your destination and/or parking or is it just mine? And you know what's worse is that I find myself doing the same. I pulled into a neighborhood where I was looking for an address of a friend's house I had never been to and what do I do? Turn my radio down so I can better concentrate. I'll be honest, my parking skills are subpar so to better help me focus, I also need, or at least feel as though I need to, to turn my music down. Tell me I'm not the only daughter who has inherited this trait from their father. Please, tell me. It's funny the things you subconsciously pick up on over the years. It's not like I ever really took note of my dad doing these things, well minus the always backing into a parking spot which we would make fun of because we weren't sure if he was looking to always be able to make a quick escape or what. Yet when I find myself doing them, I know exactly where I got them.

Imagine it's the 1990s and you are entertaining. Your guests are dressed to the nines and ready to party. All they need now are some hors d'oeuvres and a beverage. You proudly offer them some of your finest boxed wine.

What words or memories come to mind when someone mentions boxed wine? Cheapo? Flashbacks of college hangovers? Each person probably has their own opinions about it, but this is yet another example of something else I came into because of him.

This man has been drinking boxed wine since before boxed wine was cool. Long before that. I'm talking when it was pretty much socially unacceptable to drink that around others and absolutely not acceptable to serve that to others. Because boxed wine is now cool, award-winning and acceptable, or at least not frowned upon, I think he believes he was ahead of the curve. A trendsetter even. Of course, we kids don't give him the notoriety or credit he's looking for with this. We love giving him a hard time and we simply call it how we saw it; we didn't have a lot of extra money growing up and boxed wine was the cheapest. Wouldn't you know it, I now have an affinity for boxed wine. Go figure.

I'm a kid. It's late in the morning on a Saturday. I wake up to the smell of something cooking. The aroma is appealing although mixed with some unfamiliar smells I can't quite pinpoint. I walk into the kitchen to find my dad making pancakes. SCORE!

One of my favorite childhood memories with him is when he would make our family pancakes. Are you thinking how yummy this sounds? Sometimes, yes. Sometimes, no. You see, the trick with these pancakes was that he would use random ingredients. They were surprise pancakes, if you will. I absolutely love surprises but maybe not as much when they are related to food. I'd wake up and notice that the kiwis that were in the kitchen before I went to bed are now suspiciously missing. Or the papaya I knew we hadn't eaten was now possibly the orange hue standing out in my breakfast meal. He wouldn't discriminate with the ingredients; they would consist of whatever we had in the house. And I'm pretty sure he never made a specific trip to the grocery store to buy these ingredients. Whatever he wanted to use in the fridge or pantry and he wouldn't tell us what was included. Then, we would have to guess what all was in it.

Now, he wouldn't be gross and use canned tuna fish or something bizarre like that, but he would put strange fruits and spices in them for sure. Plums, apricots, pears, allspice, ginger, you get the picture. But there would never be mangos. You may be wondering why. Well, let me tell you.

Picture a man sitting under the shade of a mango tree in Fiji. The island breeze dancing on his skin. It's the perfect temperature and Robert and a buddy are having a few beers. But after one beer becomes five and a few mangos become 20, his face begins to swell up and he realizes he is having an allergic reaction. They rush to the hospital where he stays a couple of days and finds out that he is highly allergic to the sap from the mango tree. File that under things a person can be allergic to. Who knew?

Back to the pancakes.

Sometimes they were very delicious (I would actually love to eat some right now). Other times, they weren't the best and you'd just have to drench them in syrup and grin and bear it. But it was always an adventure. Always fun to be crowned the pancake ingredient guessing queen or king.

That's a good way to put a lot of things with my dad, an adventure. I've traveled to unorthodox places like Bosnia and Mongolia, just to name a few, to visit him. I remember many things about my trip to Mongolia but on the token of adventure, two things specifically stick out.

The first being that I was able to ride a camel. In my head, I'm thinking this would be similar to riding a horse. I had done that a handful of times and had enjoyable experiences. But what I didn't comprehend was how much bigger a camel was than any horse I had ever ridden.

I'm in the middle of the Mongolian desert. The wind is whipping and a unique smell begins to permeate the area. Up walk the camels, along with our guides. Here's where the situation starts to shift from my perceived expectations to reality.

The way you get onto a camel was much different than how you mount a horse. The camel kneels onto the ground, you climb on, and then he/she stands up. At that moment this was happening I realized how tall this animal was. Now, I'm not afraid of heights but I can be worried about things that are out of my control and at the moment the camel is stumbling onto its feet and I'm grasping onto whatever part of it I can, I realized I very much lacked control in this situation. Nonetheless, we slowly walked around the desert, wind attacking my face and making me chillier than I already was (never having been to Mongolia, I had no idea what to pack and clearly did not pack appropriately). But I survived and even have moments in which I enjoyed the ride. I have a photo with me on its back, crouching over grasping on for dear life and trying to smile and be warm at the same time, as a memento.

For me, there is hardly anything better than going to a spa. The euphoria begins as soon as you open the door to enter. You walk in and the smell of lavender and eucalyptus flows into your nostrils. The smell immediately goes to your head simultaneously causing you to totally relax. And that's simply the beginning.

Now, whenever I travel anywhere, I like to blend in or at least not completely stick out like a sore thumb. Try to dress appropriately and speak the native language but knowing I'd have the comfort of my dad guiding me around who could speak Mongolian fluently, I didn't come as prepared as I would if I were traveling on my own. The Mongolian language is unlike any language I was familiar with before going and not a language in which I would say is easy to pick up. Basic greetings and polite sentiments were about as far as I got. So, when I walked into a massage parlor, I didn't know what I was getting myself into.

Here comes the treatment portion of the journey.

I absolutely loveeeee getting massages and the going rate for one there was very inexpensive so, naturally, I signed up. My dad helped me get checked in and situated, as he had been there before and knew what to expect. And then, of course, left me alone to get my treatment done. Now, when I get a massage, I like some pressure to it. I don't need to feel like someone is just gently caressing my skin, I want to feel like they're getting the knots out of my muscles and releasing any tension I'm holding onto. But, on the flip side, I don't want to walk out of any spa with bruises. That, my friend, is pretty much what happened. This was the firmest massage I have ever received. I'm in there and they start with hot stones. Yes, I said they, meaning more than one person. That sounds great, right? All of this is starting off lovely. But then it quickly escalates into fist pounding and standing on my back and a whirlwind of sensations in which I have no idea how to control. I have no idea how to say in Mongolian that softer would be preferred and that they're hurting me. I also don't want to offend the massage therapist, so I pretty much just grit my teeth and bear it. Maybe this was why it was only a half-hour massage. Any longer and your body just couldn't handle it. Needless to say, I woke up the next morning feeling very sore. I suppose it was good for my tight muscles though?

As I mentioned with my dad's background and career in international development, he often lived out of the States and away from our family. I won't lie and say that was easy, but I will say that some of my love for traveling and exploring different countries and cultures I'm sure stem, at least partly, from this. That is absolutely a win. I've eaten Ethiopian food in Washington D.C., a fish eye in Croatia. I've ridden camels and slept in Gers, or yurts as they are also called, in Mongolia. Interestingly enough, yurts are gaining popularity in the United States as a form of glamping accommodations. Oh how America is often late to catch on.

He is an extremely intelligent man. As I previously mentioned, he can speak several languages fluently. Fijian is one of them. Even Fijians currently living in Fiji don't always speak Fijian (only about half of them speak it as their first language). And he has his own TEDx Talk. Hello bragging rights! With all of his smarts, I think he thrives on being the brightest man in the room. I don't say this as an ugly comment, I say this simply as a comment and an attitude I understand. Shit, if I could be the most knowledgeable person in the room, I'd want to be too. With his big brains he has his own set of idiosyncrasies, as uber intelligent people often do. Are you now going through a list of those peeps you know in your head and their unique quirks?

Let's chat about some of these quirks, shall we?

He doesn't celebrate birthdays, which I, very much, do not support. I say that mostly jokingly but also lovingly but only because I am obsessed with my birthday as I mentioned before. I find his stance on birthdays to be a bit of an oddity considering my grandma and grandpa I mentioned above love celebrating birthdays. In fact, I truly wouldn't be surprised if when asking him his age he honestly had to think about it. While I'm not 100% positive of when he stopped wanting to celebrate birthdays or if he ever liked celebrating them, I will say that he's always mentioned that Fijians don't celebrate birthdays and with all the time he spent in Fiji, I will chalk this up to a tradition he picked up there and will forever continue. Again, not for me, but you do you, dad.

My dad despises shopping but loves a good deal and dammit, so do I. But not to his extreme. He has this lime green and pink case for his iPad and I'm pretty sure he bought it not because he loves it but because it was heavily discounted. Don't ask what kind of cellphone case he has because that would be a moot point. He doesn't have a cell, nor does he want one. He still has a landline. Most of his personal items he's probably had for years, another thing I have in common with him. I kid you not, I have sweatshirts from elementary school that I still wear. An Adidas soccer warmup suit from my 8th grade travel team. Now granted, I ended up adjusting, ahem, cutting, some of the waistband to better fit but still, the rest plays. No sport pun intended. Worst (or best?) of all, I recently, within the last handful of years, threw out a pair of underwear from Limited Too. That store doesn't even exist anymore but shout out to my 1990s kids who remember it.

Being that he likes a good deal would usually mean he won't be on the forefront of setting many trends, other than in his own mind. Often, good deals are found mainly on items most people don't want. Now, I have seen people turn things into avant-garde fads, but I'll be honest and respectfully say that probably won't be the case for him.

Nonetheless, he was one of the very first people in probably hundreds of miles of our small town in Arkansas who had a Macintosh desktop computer. My dad had a former Peace Corps volunteer friend of his who opened a computer store in the Dominican Republic. It was there that my family bought their first glorious and ginormous Mac. After my family moved back to the United States, we, of course, carried the computer with us and from then on, he was hooked on Macs and probably a bit ahead of his time. This thing was basically the size of a small fridge and could easily kill someone if it fell on them. But dammit, dad was able to say that no one else (in our area at least) had one and we know how much he loves to say that.

Similar to his clothing, and as I've touched on a few times already, my dad will eat anything. Now, I'm not sure, is this specifically a dad trait or just one of my dad's? I feel like most dads are garbage disposals and will eat their kids' leftovers, but he takes it to the next level with things he will eat. I'm not sure if this is a tastebud malfunction (maybe Ron was onto something when he mentioned his lack of working tastebuds and it's an inherited gene) or just the fact that with all his years experiencing random, various worldly cuisines he just grew accustomed to eating anything and everything. I'm pretty sure any of his grandkids could scoop some dirt and pick some flowers and tell him it's dinner they made and he would eat it up. My daughter hasn't tried that, yet, but it may be coming. I'll be sure to report back.

Because anything goes with him with fashion and with food and because he's experienced so many cultural norms and cultural differences, he tends to be fairly open and accepting. That doesn't mean he will be open with how he feels. How or what he thinks? Sure, but you have to really pry him open, or maybe try to give him a few cocktails, to have him chit-chat about his feelings. As I mentioned with Ron most likely mirroring what he expresses regarding emotions from our father, our dad probably did the same. My Grandpa Reid, like my dad, has gotten more open over the years. I've only always known my grandpa to be open with his feelings but my guess is it wasn't always like that. My Grandma Reid probably had something to do with that. Rubbed off on him a bit, I think.

Now, like many of us with our parents, there may have been things I'd like for my father to have done differently or maybe expressed to me or honest conversations I've wanted to have or questions I've wanted answered over the years. I have a strong need to understand why people do the things they do. And when that can't be explained I don't really like that. Yes, I was the kid whose constant curiosity had me incessantly asking, "Why?" Why do we need to wear panties? Why can't I get a princess Power Wheels? Why do my brothers fart so much? Why can't I balance on my head forever? Yes, I am the adult who binge watches true crime documentaries and shows like Intervention to fill my continual need for understanding people.

But even without every single question I've ever had being given what I feel is a legitimate answer, I have never worried about him being proud of me. Ever. Even to this day. His pride for his kids is practically palpable. That's an admirable trait and one that I know some people wouldn't be able to relate to. I never felt like I was trying to live up to anything to impress him with my accolades and what a relief that is. My therapy sessions dropped by 50% from that alone, I'm sure.

The open and accepting statement I made above about Robert also doesn't infer that he will be fluid with how he likes things and wants things done. He gets stuck in his ways sometimes and is very uncomfortable when things don't go accordingly. He'll go with the flow as long as he's in charge of the flow. Admittedly enough, I too can sometimes be that way. I get a little twitchy when things are out of my control. Cue an uncomfortable Stewie Griffin from *Family Guy* or Squidward Tentacles from *SpongeBob*

*SquarePant*s.

As I briefly mentioned previously, my parents divorced when I was younger. I was in elementary school. I was sad but also suggested and expected it. While I wish that, as a family, we could have found ways for my pops to fulfill his dreams and pursue what he wanted while having his family nearby, I'm not going to blame every mishap I've ever had on the fact my parents didn't stay together. Sure, it absolutely made me a sad girl. There are times when I wonder how things would have been different had they stayed together, but people go their separate ways. Things change. Splits happen. Shit happens.

Unfortunately, divorce happens. And it happens to many, many people. I think sometimes when this happens to girls, people expect you to have some sort of emotional baggage. Some sort of issues. Well, shit, don't we all, boy or girl?

It's like some people assume daddy issues are assigned as the divorce papers are finalized, as if it's Oprah handing out free gifts. You get some daddy issues, and you get some daddy issues, everybody gets some daddy issues! But, I have never in my life wanted to claim any type of daddy issues; being compared to Anna Nicole Smith or every wife Hugh Hefner has ever had. Like, just hand me the daddy issue starter kit consisting of a pole, all the wine, and an older man. Well, hmm, dang, I've got two of those things.

I have a best friend who has always affirmed her daddy issues. I don't know if, for her, it's a badge of honor in some way showing what all you've been through and still accomplished or if it's the opposite, the ability to do whatever the hell you want and act however you like while having a seemingly valid excuse. I'm not sure. Maybe it's merely because this friend of mine is a completely open book so she will let you know any and every perceived imperfection she has at all times. She's the person who will have a pimple and make sure to point it out to you first thing. As in, walk in the door and immediately draw attention to her clogged pore. It's okay, we know, we see it. But she's hysterical and I always appreciate her honesty and candidness.

Back to dads and issues we may or may not have. I never wanted to blame any person or any life situation for any of my crazy or less desirable traits. I never wanted to give anyone or anything that much credit, even if deep down, there may be some truth to adult problems and childhood upbringing. I'm sure straight-shooting Dr. Phil would love to tell us all about whether or not this correlation exists. Mostly, I probably never wanted to be associated with the stigma that I believe comes along with saying something like that either (see above situations and women I don't want to be associated with). However, I did like the quote I saw recently from a girl thanking her dad: "Dad, thanks for giving me enough emotional baggage to be in a creative field but not enough to be a prostitute." That one made me laugh.

Being an adult and having a kid now, I understand the difficult balance of wanting to keep your identity as you, the person, while also trying to maintain you, the parent. In fact, that was something I really wanted to strive for when Jeff and I decided to have kids. A lot of people find their identity in their kids and that's fine for them, but I never wanted to lose myself in another person, even if that person was my offspring. Someone who I literally created inside of me.

All these years, I've thought sometimes my dad could be selfish, when, maybe it was me, also, being a little selfish. Damn for that realization! I think we can all be quick to see our side of the story and maybe not as fast to see another way or believe another way is correct. But I think when you're a kid you feel entitled to play that self-centered card or maybe you don't know any other way to look at it. Maybe we're all a bit (or a lot) selfish and constantly figure out how to combat that and be less so. Or at least I would hope we are trying for that.

Let's be honest, many people have both their parents around their entire lives and they're just as effed up as any of us with a membership to the divorce club. We all are just trying to keep calm and carry on, I suppose.

How about we go back to funny idiosyncrasies?

For as long as I can remember, and I feel as though this trait most likely goes back for much longer than that, Robert has snapped his fingers to any song he hears. Using both his right and left hands. Creating the foundation for some sweet dance moves. And I'm talking about any and every song. And he is now adamant on teaching my daughter how to snap her fingers as well, which began pretty much as soon as she had control of her hands. I have a confession to make about snapping. It wasn't until about a handful of years ago that I learned what actually causes the snapping sound. Do you know? It's caused by the middle finger slapping the ball of the thumb. It's not simply your middle finger and thumb making the noise. The rest of the hand joins in and then the sound gets amplified by the soundwave of a tube formed by the curled little fingers. Seriously, try it. Check it out. I'll be honest, my mind was blown.

Robert isn't the guy you necessarily want to watch movies with. He doesn't remember movies so he can watch them over and over again, which is fine, but he's the guy who talks throughout the entire thing. Maybe sitting in silence is a struggle or uncomfortable to him or maybe he wants to give his opinion and know everyone else's. Regardless, that shit can wait until the end. Not for him though. My brothers and I go into watching a movie with him pretty much knowing he won't be silent the entire time. Now, my brother Ron can and will watch movies repeatedly, not because he doesn't remember, but because he simply loves them. For me, there are very few movies I want to watch repeatedly. Christmas movies like *Elf*? Sure. The entire *Terminator* series? No, that's okay. One and done all the way through (or not) is fine. Regardless, if we've seen it before or not, that doesn't mean we want to chit-chat throughout the show, but dad can't help himself. So, we give in, grab some wine, and settle in to try to enjoy it.

Do you find that the older and more grown-up you get, the more you find out about your parents? We were in Detroit visiting my grandparents a few years ago and after a few cigars and a few drinks, dad began telling me, Ron and Jeff this story about him and some of his buddies hitchhiking across Europe. Dad grew up going to a military boarding school and his dad was a judge so his world was relatively authoritarian. Not to mention that his mom, a woman who I loved very much but spent many years afraid of because she wasn't what many would call warm and fuzzy, was fairly strict as well.

With all those things and being that my dad grew up during a time of "Make love, not war", he was due to get a bit wild and let loose. So off to Europe he and his friends went. And without telling his parents, mind you. I can imagine not telling my folks plenty of things. But internationally travelling? Nah, I think that's something you sort of have to do. Now, at the time, they were poor college students. They got by how they could, which included hitchhiking.

In my eyes, hitchhiking has never seemed like a good idea, so why is it that we hear of stories from decades ago where people did this all willy-nilly? It was common. It's not as though there were less crazies around and less trouble people could get into. As a matter of fact, it's probably safer to hitchhike now, now that we have tracking on pretty much every device we own and are rarely without someone else knowing our whereabouts.

I suppose that's neither here nor there, people did it back then and that's how our story starts. Poor college kids. In Europe. Trying to get around. They hopped on freight trains and snuck from railway station to railway station and then hitchhiked when their luck on trains ran out or they needed to get where the trains weren't running. Never fell into any trouble, however, Robert and his pal, we'll call him Jude, did end up getting separated from each other. My dad stayed in Greece or some other seaside country to hang out with a woman he met. Jude carried on. Now, of course, this was before the days of commonplace cell phones. They took the approach and had the understanding that they'd simply see each other when they saw each other again. Not to worry. No big deal. This, I believe, occurred because they were men. Women, I don't believe, would do this. Most women I know wouldn't separate from their friend in a foreign country. But the boys did and they didn't bother figuring out where they'd be next or write to each other or conjure up any ideas of how to keep in touch. They just went on their merry little ways. Months later, still in Europe, Robert and Jude had a serendipitous reencounter and reconnected. Robert saw Jude from across a park. Jude was mingling and speaking with a group of Hare Krishnas. Whether he was now a follower in this religious group, I am not sure. But I do know he had made friends with them. At the moment my dad was approaching, Jude was literally chatting with them about Robert! Life is funny. I suppose it may have been the universe's way of bringing them back together. Robert and Jude are friends to this day.

Nowadays Robert lives the retired life on a small island in Washington with his wife but stays busy and active putzing around their house and sitting on the board of various nonprofit organizations, continuing to work to his heart's content by helping with international development. He's even roped Ron, Anna, Jeff and me into being on the board for the nonprofit he created called Waivunia, The Island Development Initiative. Okay, no, he didn't coerce us, we were happy to be a part of this great cause and it's been a neat family thing to participate in together. Waivunia is focused on helping make rural island communities better and happier. In fact, the first project we completed helped the village Sonny lives in. He still calls me sweetie, gives the best hugs, and I'm pretty sure he often wears sandals with socks. So, I'll leave you with that lovely visual.

LESSONS LEARNED:

- Travel all over the world. Go to the popular hotspots, sure, but also experience places you'd call random and see what they have to offer.
- Learn new languages and teach them to your children, if you have any.
- Never stop learning. There's no such thing as being too smart.
- Don't be afraid to lay it all out on the table. Say how you feel. Talk about your feelings. Express your feelings and express yourself to those closest to you.
- Cook pancakes for your family or friends and make mealtime with them fun. Whether you want to use random ingredients from your fridge or pantry is up to you, but make it enjoyable and memorable.
- Wear whatever the heck you want.

CHAPTER NINE

MORE-THAN-MEETS-THE-EYE MOM

Let me set the stage for Mary, my mom. She is by far the kindest person I've ever met. The most selfless and caring and empathetic. She's the person who knows what you need and doesn't make you wait for it or even ask for it. She simply gives people what they need.

Don't misinterpret these incredibly lovely traits for someone who is a softy. She speaks her mind, says her truths, and stands her ground. She has been referred to as firm but fair many times in her professional life. She is the definition of a boss lady, running nursing homes for the last few decades and doing a damn good job at it. She's a social worker by trade, graduating from Bemidji State University (go Beavers!). She left the small towns where she spent her life and joined the Peace Corps, which sent her to Grenada, Jamaica, and the Dominican Republic, and she's traveled to numerous other places.

Her time in Jamaica led to her love of reggae music, which I very much appreciate that she likes. I like it because it's seemingly out of the norm for moms to jam to reggae. That being said, she does also love what you would imagine moms liking, like Sarah McLachlan and James Taylor. Fleetwood Mac is a popular choice as well. And for whatever reason, whenever I hear Dan Fogelberg, I think of her. When I was younger, I would give her CDs for gifts (now I've upgraded to concert tickets). Ones like the

Grey's Anatomy soundtrack. A decision to this day that I stand by because, while that show has lost its luster, their music selection hasn't. Yet, I still watch the damn series because at this point I'm invested in it and I have to see it through to the bitter end.

I read a magazine article years ago in its Mother's Day edition in which people shared what their mothers had taught them over the years. One person, and I have no idea why this has stuck with me over the years but it's probably because I thought it was so random and unimpressive, said that her mom taught her how to groom her eyebrows. Like seriously?! I mean, that is important, sure, but even in a beauty magazine, you can't think of something a little more meaningful other than the plucking, shaping and/or coloring of your eyebrows? Maybe I'm just bitter because we know that I have practically nonexistent eyebrows so there's not much to work with when it comes to someone helping me with them. The biggest takeaway this mother gave, for anyone who is interested, was to not pluck above your eyebrows, only underneath. Earth-shattering? I'm not sure but do with it what you want. Anyway, I don't need to get off on health or beauty tips.

My mom has three signature statements which are on constant rotation in my head. One is "When someone shows you who they are, believe them." Meaning, don't try to make excuses for people and don't try to change them. People are who they are. She believes the best in people but how often do we excuse or justify the actions of others because we want them to be a certain way or we don't want to believe who they truly are? Yeah, don't do that.

Her other go-to statement: "It'll be fine." She says this with a nonchalant hand gesture and a smile. Jeff even knows this one well and often imitates her.

Thirdly, "You always have a choice." This remark from her is both empowering and also intimidating. You always have a choice of choosing a different direction for your life. You always have a choice of choosing how you react to situations. You always have a choice. In life. With everything.

I mentioned I got my love for holding onto items for an overly extended period of time from my dad, but it's also a trait my mom has as well. Mary loves sweatshirts. That's almost always her go-to souvenir. Who doesn't love a good sweatshirt? They're cozy and comfy and usually they only get better with age. But she has this one sweatshirt. It's light pink and plain. Nothing on it except for some stains. It's oversized but not in a trendy or flattering way that petite women like herself can sometimes pull off. She bought it at a yard sale for $.25 and she's had it for almost as long as I've been alive. That's the sweatshirt she wears the most and she most likely won't retire it until she absolutely has to. Until it has holes. Actually, I believe it already has holes so that means she probably won't get rid of it until it literally falls apart. Until it disintegrates off her body. When I see her in it, we both laugh because I've given her crap so many times and she knows what I'd say. But truth be told, we both know I don't have a leg to stand on with how I also hold onto things.

I had a shirt from a guy I liked in high school (it was a hand-me-down from him, nothing more scandalous or anything that you may be thinking). It was a Ninja Turtles shirt that was one of the softest t-shirts I owned. I cut it to make it off the shoulder and wore that thing for years. I wore it until the neck continued to get bigger and I could barely wear it without exposing a boob and until the holes in it grew to be too much.

So, I get it. One other sweatshirt she has is one she found in our cabin up north. It was presumably her dad's, my Grandpa Chet's, so again, it's oversized and comfy, just how she wants it. It has a picture of a wolf on it with a description underneath discussing this Canadian species. It's one that she should be wearing at the cabin, around a fire, lounging, but nowhere else. It's not what one would call cute. I hope you have a lovely image in your head. But the kicker, even more than the great large picture of the wolf, is the fact that the description is full of misspelled words and grammatical errors. I know many Canadians are native speakers of French but even something that was lost in translation from French to English cannot be an accurate explanation of all that is wrong with this sweatshirt's verbiage. But I know, especially since it holds sentimental value because it's Mary's dad's, that she won't ever let it go. I'm okay with it being a standing joke we pass onto future generations.

Back to the topic of yard sales. Mary loves them. She gets this from her mama, Grandma Pat, and I get it from her. Maybe it's for the simple reason that she is looking to strike gold on another pink Fruit of the Loom sweatshirt deal or just likes the thrill of the chase and the digging through of knick-knacks. Our three generations have gone to many a sale in our day and always find something to bring home.

I think this is something you either love or hate. Lots of people I know don't want to buy other people's used things but we are the people that find treasures in the trash. What's funny is my mom loathes stores like the Dollar Store or T.J. Maxx. I suppose she wants to separate her shopping into categories. One category is when you score an unreal deal on previously loved items and know you will have to dig for the diamond in the rough sometimes. The other category is when she wants to buy something new and nicer and cut out the time it takes to dig and quickly get to the item she wants to purchase. In one category she probably is only browsing for things that pique her interest and in the other she is on a mission to find a specific item. In the latter case, she doesn't want to dig or deal with what she perceives as clutter and random odds and ends. Usually, I would categorize the person who likes yard or garage sales to be the same person who likes discount retailers, not her. To each their own.

Some things, other than discounted retail stores, she doesn't like include Styrofoam and when her children and children-in-law won't stop quoting movies. The Styrofoam hatred stems from the fact it's awful for the environment. It can't be recycled and never disintegrates. I think she also hates the way it sounds and feels. The movie quotes, she can never keep up with. She says that her brain doesn't work like that. I guess she means that it doesn't retain stupid stuff like ours do. We could have full blown conversations using only movie or television quotes (it's truly a fun game you should try sometime) and she'll laugh at our stupidity but rarely be able to guess the movie or join in. Eventually she just walks away, unable to handle our ridiculousness. But like Mary, we all have our things.

MORE-THAN-MEETS-THE-EYE MOM

She's pretty much the epitome of everything good in this world (or at least, certainly, in my life), but she's not all sweet and innocent.

Let me tell you about her first love of her life. She met him when she was in college. He lived in her hometown in North Dakota and they met when she was home for the summer during break. She knew of him because he was a friend of her uncle. At this time, he was out of college and working as a business consultant. He had previously gone to college, or university as they call it overseas, in Denmark and spent time playing professional hockey. While he was there, he got arrested for drugs. Mary's dad said everyone makes mistakes and everyone brushed it off not thinking too much about it. By the time she started hanging out with him it was water under the bridge. So yes, she knew this history but never suspected anything. She believed he was a good guy, which he was, and off their story goes. She tells it as almost a love at first sight type of thing. They met and were shortly inseparable. They would cook fun meals together, go camping, explore old abandoned farm houses, play games, and hang out with each other's friends. And even though they lived over two hours away from each other, with her in Bemidji, Minnesota and him in Grand Forks, North Dakota, they saw each other often. With his job, he was around plenty of bigwigs and smart folks. They spent time with well-known lawyers and business executives. But this love story does have an unexpected twist.

As it turns out, the entire time they were dating he was dealing hashish, or hash as it's more commonly known. Yes, you heard right, he was a drug dealer and, believe it or not, an international drug dealer at that. He was importing hash from Syria and selling it all over the United States and Canada. Often to those notable bigshots I told you about.

Okay, so this isn't the 1970s anymore and I feel like we rarely hear about hash. It's the resin of the female cannabis plant that has been separated from the plant itself. Whereas weed, is the dried, unprocessed flowers of the female cannabis plant. Apparently, hash is the most potent form of the cannabis plant because the extraction process rids extraneous things in the plant and gets straight to the point of getting high. Okay, so now that we have gone over some basic drug facts, back to the story.

My mom is a child of the 1970s so to say she never tried any drugs would be to lie to you and while she was a bit of a hippie in her time (a trait that I inherited as well...ah, how I wish I was a 1970s baby), she was never big into drugs or alcohol.

My mom wants to see and believe the best in everyone, but she's not naïve, and they did go to parties together, but she truly never remembers or saw any suspicious behavior and never saw him do any drugs. They would occasionally drink at parties but that's it. Again, she had no reason to think anything was happening behind her back, or, as it happened, in front of her face. He and his buddies were smuggling the hash in through backgammon boards. Many of those smart, interesting, bigwigs they hung with often bought their drugs from them. Did I mention they played backgammon together? He taught her how to play and she very much enjoyed the game. To this day, I'm sure she can never play the game or look at the board the same. Well, as

MORE-THAN-MEETS-THE-EYE MOM

chance would have it, unfortunately, they got busted. They had been dating for about five months at this time and he was supposed to be on his way to visit her at college when her mom called her and asked if she had seen the news. Mary told her she hadn't and grandma suggested she may want to turn it on because her boyfriend had just been involved in the largest drug bust in the state of North Dakota.

A few days before the raid, the Drug Enforcement Agency (DEA) in Grand Forks was given a tip from the Royal Canadian Mounted Police (yes, that is a real thing). The tip came from wiretapped phone conversations in Canada and Austria regarding a suspected drug transaction at a local hotel. The DEA staked out the hotel for days and began following their suspects, one of which, of course, was my mom's then boyfriend. He'd pull up with his trunk and pull-behind camper (remember the camping they enjoyed together?) and they followed him back to his apartment. The federal agents saw her boyfriend and his roommate at the time using saws and hammers and working on wooden boxes which they loaded, along with a gun case, into the truck. Those wooden boxes were the almost 200 backgammon boards which were shipped from Syria. After it looked like their work was done and he went to take the hotel guest to the airport, the officers made their arrest.

He had a jury trial that lasted nine days, which she went to, and he was sentenced to 12 years in prison for two drug-related crimes and one charge of unlawfully carrying a firearm during the commission of a felony. He ended up only serving a handful of years. They tried to keep in touch for months via snail mail but she wasn't about to wait for him. She was off to the Peace Corps to start her "real" adult life. They both had this understanding, notion, assumption, or whatever you would like to call it that they would reconnect.

Many years later, her dad passed away and she was back in her hometown. She ran into him for the first time since the sentencing. They talked and judging by how she tells the story, the spark still could have been there. But at this time, they were both married with children and their lives had taken them down different paths. They never saw each other again after that.

In the winter of 2017, he was walking his dog outside in the snow and the dog ran onto a frozen lake and fell in. He tried to rescue the dog and ended up drowning. People talk of his love for the outdoors and the passion he had for life. He was a pilot and a gardener and ended up starting a business that provided in-home care for the elderly and disabled. He was obviously very smart, to run a scheme like that you have to be. You'd also have to be a bit adventurous or daring, for simple terms, or, to put it in more blunt terms (marijuana pun not intended), ballsy. And he was clearly a dog lover. He was only 70 years old when he passed. To this day, she remembers and talks of him fondly and, in fact, not to put words in her mouth, he was probably one of her greatest loves to this day (I say that with no disrespect and without slight to my dad or stepdad). It's interesting to think of how different their lives could have been had he not gotten caught.

MORE-THAN-MEETS-THE-EYE MOM

Did I mention I only recently, as in a year ago, found all this out?? Reading this book will be the first time many of her friends or family will hear of it.

To completely change the subject, did anyone else's mothers want to match and then take glamour shot style professional pictures? Anyone?? Well in case it's just mine, let me tell you a little bit about these outfits. The look often had the theme of the louder and bolder the print, the better. I can vividly remember a floral printed jumpsuit for me and a dress for mom, consisting of hot pink, bright blue, and shades of greens. These were large flowers I'm talking about too, nothing subtle. As I got older, I would poke fun at how my mom wanted to match and do these photoshoots but dang it, now that I have a daughter, I, too, want to partake in the sweetness of matching outfits with her. To this day, Mary still enjoys matching but now it's with the entire family and in the form of Christmas PJs.

My mom started rubbing my feet when I was a baby. I get it. I understand the strong urge to want to love on baby feet. Little baby feet are so cute and sweet and are practically begging to be rubbed but she continued as I got older. Well, now I'm over 30 and still when I go home to visit, I almost always ask for a foot rub. I swore to myself when I had kids that I wouldn't start this habit. For one, I hate feet. Despise them. Think they're gross even if they've been freshly cleaned. I don't like anyone except her and the employees at a nail salon to touch my feet. Honestly, I am only now, over the last few years, allowing my husband to touch my feet and we've been together for over 12 years. And for two, I do not want to be a slave to my grownup children who after years of raising them and putting them first should be rubbing my feet not the other way around (see my first note which I probably wouldn't allow anyway). My mom is so selfless that she may not see it this way but just take my word for it, if you haven't already started a habit, don't. You're welcome.

Some of my favorite times in my life have been spent playing games with my mom and my entire family, both immediate and extended. We all absolutely love game night. We have for as long as I can recall. I remember growing up playing all sorts of games: Pretty, Pretty Princess (which my daughter now plays), Candy Land, Monopoly (when someone would invest the long time it would take to finish the game), a variety of matching games, dominos, chess (I actually am a wicked chess player, even won a tournament in my day), checkers, cards, Bop It (when no one wanted to play a game with me), and so many more. As we've grown up, the games have gotten more advanced and even a little mature (hello Cards Against Humanity), except when there are children involved, but the joy and fun and overall experience of togetherness has remained the same. Games aren't just for children. They're meant for anyone, no matter how old, looking to put a little laughter into their day or night (Lord knows we've had many late nights playing games).

One game night tradition we have is on New Year's Eve. NYE is one of my absolute favorite holidays. I love the idea of new beginnings and new goals and the fresh start a new year seems to bring. And while I love dressing up and having a nice dinner out on the town and really being around the energy of others celebrating the evening, I also love the idea of bringing that experience home. So, for a handful of New Year's Eve celebrations we've done just that. We've gotten dressed up (as much as each person would like), cooked a fancy dinner, and celebrated, at home, together and this celebration always includes games. We'll usually stop to watch a ball drop and do a countdown or view fireworks out the windows and then get right back into whatever game we're engrossed in. Whether at my mom's house or my own, friends, family, all are welcome and we've loved kicking off the fresh year with loved ones.

Remember me mentioning a cop car story about the time I was dropped off at my Grandma Pat's house with my two friends? More on that now. The cops got a hold of us as we were leaving a party and we couldn't hide the fact we had been drinking and busted we were. They hand out MIP's (minor in possession) up in North Dakota like they're candy at Halloween, so, wanting to assure nothing would show up on any of our records, we hired a local lawyer to help us out. The lawyer we hired was someone my mom went to high school with so he really enjoyed that, not that she did. Years later, while attending my mom's 40th high school reunion back up north, I saw him again. I was wearing this black and white jumpsuit and he died laughing and made, what he thought, was the funniest comparison reference to a prison jumpsuit. Guess I deserved that.

My mom never punished to make a point or to simply express her authority and never said things like "Because I said so" or "I told you so." She never cried over spilt milk or accidents. She would always explain herself. With my tendencies to ask why and always wanting to know the reasoning behind decisions, this was important and probably in a way comforting to me. We never got spankings, not that my brothers and I were angels. We were absolutely not. She and my dad just didn't believe in that form of physical punishment. I, too, am uncomfortable with it and find it a bit hard to wrap my head around. "Hey kid, don't hit people now come over here and let me give you a spanking." Hmm. Anyway, she would discipline us because she generally cared and would say things like "I'm not mad, I'm disappointed." For some reason, that cuts like a dagger more than anything else that can be done or said. I got into plenty of trouble in high school, as many of us do, but the time I remember most, the time that cut the deepest is when I came home after drinking. I couldn't, and still can't, hold my alcohol. Smell it, practically get drunk, as I mentioned previously. I'm a lightweight, as in I only need the pre-game, not the actual game. But even with knowing this, drinking games were always appealing and keeping up with others just seemed like a good thing to try at the time. Both trends I continued to regret up until my late 20s, but I'm learning (count your drinks, eat plenty, don't try to keep up with your husband who is much larger and with a much higher tolerance than you)!

Back to the story. I came home that night and it was very clear I would be in trouble. I had taken it entirely too far. The alcohol had, once again, gotten the better of me. She didn't bother reprimanding me that evening but the next morning I remember her coming into my room and starting to cry when she began saying how I was her best friend and she doesn't know what she would do if something bad ever happened to me. Cue all the tears then and now, especially after having my own kid and understanding her sentiment. Then of course, as she would repetitively do, she sentenced me to a day spent cleaning the entire house. While hungover (and you remember how miserably awful my hangovers are and I'm sure that day I was taking breaks to go barf in the bathroom). The combination of her words and the punishment was hell on earth. Disappointing her was harder than any other sentence I'd have to serve. I will especially remember the deep cleaning of the house punishment for my own kids though. That's a good one. She was also big on grounding us from friends and anything fun and taking away phone or computer privileges. The latter part of that didn't impact my brothers as much since they didn't spend lots of time on our landline or have things like social media on our first computer, i.e., the largest Mac ever created.

Growing up my parents drank on occasion but it was never a part of daily life, at least that I can remember, and they certainly were not the type to go out to bars or parties. As I got a little older, I actually wished my parents would do more with friends, thinking it would be good for them to increase their social activities. I still believe this but also respect wanting to be a homebody as I so often am. Alcohol wasn't something idolized. They weren't partying nonstop or chugging beers on the regular. And it wasn't something forbidden, as in drink one sip and you'll go to hell (we grew up Methodists, not Baptists, after all) but it was common with many extended family members. I suppose when you're young and figuring things out and awkward and want something to help, you experiment how those around you are experimenting. The older people I hung out with and my best girlfriends were all interested in alcohol. Now, I know we can't change the past and maybe it leads us to where we are today and who were supposed to be and blah, blah, blah and all that but all of my biggest regrets and largest hardships come from drinking. I was always a straight A kid, always on honor roll, and never let those unbeneficial weekend extracurriculars get in the way of getting my shit done but damn did it cause me head and heart aches (literally and figuratively) and many unnecessary punishments. That is a lesson I tried to teach my younger stepsister over the years (now she has a medical marijuana card and prefers not to drink at all, although I think that's just her preference and not my doing) and one that I will teach my kids.

To bring this back to a more lighthearted matter, one of the funniest stories of this debauchery was during a night we went to a friend's beach condo for a party they were having. I, once again, didn't know my limit so my girlfriends who were staying with me and trying to cover up the alcohol that had been consumed, were trying to find tricks to make it seem as though you haven't been drinking or ways to sober up. They landed on mustard.

Now I don't know who told them that yellow mustard, yes, the kind you use for sandwiches, would be able to mask the smell or have some magical sobering qualities but our ride took us to the gas station, we bought some, and we proceeded to squirt it into my mouth all the way home until we were practically walking up the stairs into my house. No surprise here, it didn't work. We still got busted by Mary and, you guessed it, we all cleaned the house the next day. Can't always easily take the wild out of the child. Side note, if anyone has any scientific evidence regarding yellow mustard and its effects on alcohol, please let me know.

I don't remember either one of my parents cursing growing up. Or my brothers. To this day, the four of them rarely curse. So, I'm not really sure where my sailor-esque tendencies come from. Previously, my mother despised the F-word. I say previously because, while, she still doesn't love it, I've actually heard her say it now a handful of times and this is shocking to me; as it is something I never thought would happen. When my daughter was only beginning to talk, we were changing her and she dropped the toy she was holding onto off her changing table and said, "Shit." My husband looked at me and shook his head, knowing she picked this up from me and while I don't want some children cursing, we were both impressed she used the word in the correct context. I'll start being more concerned when she says my favorite curse word, the F-bomb. A lot of people tell their children that those are bad words and I'm not pretending they're good words but I think I like the phrase that those are adult words. Now, if I was being the good Christian I try to be, I would work on taming my tongue altogether, and I do, but sometimes it just feels good to say the F-word. Anyone else with me; anyone else feel the same??

It's Friday night, which means movie night with the fam. You walk into Blockbuster, the smell of videos and what feels like infinite possibilities flood your nostrils. The excitement is in the air. What's new on the shelves? What will you end up going home with to watch? You and your family agree on a movie (or two) and stroll over to the checkout counter where you wait your turn (it's busy on a Friday night) and are reminded of the large variety of treats for purchase.

Now, let me pause here and introduce you to something that Mary taught our family and me. It's the Law of Attraction, which states that positive or negative thoughts bring like thoughts into existence. If you expect the best, then that will happen, expect the opposite, well you can attract that too. Why am I bringing this up while discussing Blockbuster? What do Blockbuster and the Law of Attraction have in common? Nik-L-Nip wax bottle candies. I learned about and first believed in the power of the Law of Attraction with those candies.

Now, back to the checkout line. We'd usually buy Twizzlers (Mary's favorite) and I, for whatever reason, always loved those little wax bottles. We'd get home and while watching our new release, I'd bite off the top of the wax bottle and drink the sugary liquid inside. I would then cover my teeth with the wax from the candy and pretend I had retainers. I can't tell you how many times I did this. Well, the joke is on me. I have retainers that I've worn since I got my braces off in elementary school which I will need to wear the rest of my life to keep my teeth in line. Real cute when I climb in bed with my husband. Not quite as much fun as pretending with Nik-L-Nips. Maybe I wished this upon myself, but I do believe the Law of Attraction is a real thing.

I even attracted a man, my now husband, after Mary encouraged me to visualize and speak aloud what I was wanting in a partner. We were walking on the beach one day after I had experienced a lovely (that's sarcasm) breakup. She asked if I could list all the traits I would want to have in my next partner. On a whim, I recited a list of qualities (someone who was close with his family and would become close to mine, someone who was fun and funny, someone who was smart, someone who had a strong faith, etc.) I would like in the next person I would date and low and behold, very shortly afterwards Jeff and I started dating and you know how the rest of our story goes. Listen, even if the Law of Attraction, or whatever term you'd like to give this occurrence, isn't real, wouldn't we rather think for the best and hope positive things come to fruition? It sure beats the alternative. But I say, if Murphy's Law, stating if anything can go wrong, it will, is a thing many people believe it then we dang sure can believe the opposite.

Mary also taught me that often the things that come naturally to us are our gifts. The things we assume everyone is good at or excels at. Many times though, those are our own unique talents. Ones that we shouldn't overlook or take for granted. Believe these things. Believe that you are special. That there's no one else quite like you. If no one else believes you are or believes in you, call up Mary, she'll give you the pep talk you need. She's a born trainer. Teacher. It's not surprising her background is in social work because she truly wants to help people develop themselves and empower them and improve their overall well-being.

Returning back to how this chapter started, if I were to give a statement, proclamation, or revelation to a beauty magazine on something my mother has taught me other than to always wash your face and your makeup brushes (rules it may have taken me into my late twenties to finally abide by, but it is very important, especially for women), it would be to simply, although more often easier said than done, take care of yourself. Whatever that means to you. Whatever self-care looks like for you. Maybe it's taking a bath (very much a Mary thing to do but not for me). Maybe it's trying yoga. My mom and I began practicing yoga when I was in my early teens and it truly is life-changing. It can and will transform your body, your mind, your soul if you let it. And if nothing else you move and stretch your body and you can never do that too much. Maybe it's axe throwing to relieve all of your frustrations. Maybe it's sitting in silence or jamming aloud to gangster rap you secretly only listen to when you're alone in your car. Maybe it's eating a PB&J while you walk around your house in a fluffy robe. Maybe it's buying a houseplant or flowers for yourself. It can be anything. I'm not judging and no one else will either. Just do something you love every day and be nice to yourself.

Oh, and don't wear jewelry to bed. This has been instilled in my head since I was a kid. My mom never let me wear jewelry to sleep. Even now, to this day, I won't sleep in any of my jewels except for sometimes my wedding ring. I know she simply didn't want me wearing a necklace and silently choking to death in the middle of the night. Smart. Good parenting. And I'm not sure if it's the fear from that that I subconsciously think about or merely the fact I find it uncomfortable now (or do I find it uncomfortable because I have an underlying thought of impending doom?) but regardless, it's a rule I still follow.

LESSONS LEARNED:

- Always focus on the positives.
- Know that you always have a choice.
- Remember that you can never be too kind. Mary is the type of person who makes everything okay. Any of my perceived flaws, insecurities, shortcomings, she always makes me feel worthy or whole or good enough and that is something that I pray to inherit as a mom, a spouse, and/or a friend. Be the person who calms the anxieties of others. Be the person who, through your kindness, makes the lives of others better, whether it's through your career or your general way of living.
- Try your best, if at all possible, to avoid dating drug dealers.
- If you haven't already, don't start rubbing your kids' feet.

And if you have already picked up this habit, stop it as quickly as you can.

CHAPTER TEN
ENTERTAINING TOT

Speaking of the opposite of taking care of yourself. Try having a kid (I guess the perk is maybe they'll take care of you when you're older). Pfeiffer Mackenzie or PMack as we fondly call her for short, is our two-and-a-half-year-old daughter. Our first, and at this time, our only born.

Before she was born, I thought I knew love. I loved my parents, my family, my friends, and of course, Jeff. That was the capacity I had and knew for love and I thought that was great. Tremendous. But once we had her, we felt a love we had never experienced before. I never knew my heart could feel so deeply, could be so big. I didn't know those depths were possible.

I know I am not the only parent who thinks this but wanted to highlight how truly incredible it is. Before we had her, after realizing I even wanted to have kids at all, we knew we would have more than one. I am not what one would call a kid person. I didn't grow up babysitting little ones and loving on any and every child I saw. No, that's not me at all. I never knew I wanted any, actually, quite the opposite, I didn't truly think I would want to take a dive into that deep end. Shoot, I didn't even know if I'd end up getting married (and I definitely wouldn't have gone down the road of children without that).

But I believe if you're going to venture down the path of having any at all then you've got to have more than one. Let me be honest, most of the only children I know are selfish or lack certain social skills, not to mention, having siblings is just fun. Think about it, think about some of the only children you know. What are they like? I don't want to say I told you so but I'm going to assume you came to the realization I did.

After having Pfeiffer and once again, not feeling as though it was possible for my heart to get any bigger, I can now absolutely see how parents are happy and content and overjoyed with keeping their child count to a singular number. I told Jeff, if for some reason we can't have any more kids, I will be more than just okay with it. I will feel complete still. And to be honest, she's so good, we have been nervous about rolling the dice again, just assuming our next will be a hellion little shit.

Ultimately, we did want her to have a sibling and to have another kid. One of my good girlfriends said something to me a few years or so ago when I was telling her all the things I just mentioned above and what she said was groundbreaking to me. She said that when you have another child, you don't have to share your love, rather, your heart actually grows. Grows more?! How is that possible?! But she has two kiddos so I know it's the truth. Sometimes it's the simple things that people say that impact us so profoundly. So, we took the plunge and here we are with baby number two on the way.

I wanted a boy initially and when I was pregnant, I truly thought Pfeiffer was a boy. I suppose it was possibly simply my deep desires tricking me and making me believe I had that voodoo mother's intuition, cause I clearly, did not. I am happy to report that baby two will be a boy. Hope this isn't a situation of needing to be careful what you wish for.

Now, to chat a bit more on names. It never dawned on me that people could confuse her first and last name until lately. I mean the name you give someone holds a lot of weight and we didn't take it lightly, running through how it sounded separately and as a whole, and what her initials looked like together. Yes, please forgive me, I'm from the south, land of all things monogrammed so the way the initials work together is a somewhat important factor.

All in all, we really never thought someone could think Bell was her first name and Pfeiffer was her last name. Oops. Oh well. But it makes sense. Pfeiffer is a family name. It is Jeff's maternal grandfather's mother's maiden name. We fell in love with this name and it was a much better choice than the name of another one of his ancestor's, Kunigunda. We had one other name picked out, this was the name we chose. The name she most looked like. She will also have a heck of a time learning to spell her name. Right now, she knows her name starts with a P but clearly Pfeiffer doesn't sound like a P word. We liked it more than we cared about her struggles with it or maybe we just knew she could get through it since Jeff and I both have somewhat tricky name situations. He is a junior so people have continued to call him the wrong name, and misspell Jeffrey, his entire life and people hardly ever spell Erika correctly or my maiden name of Reid so we know she can handle it. It was too pretty, unique, catchy, and meaningful of a name not to go for it. So, I'm sorry we're not sorry little PMack.

As I briefly mentioned, Pfeiffer is a good kid. And I won't bore you with this section because Lord knows I don't really care to hear about all the great things other people's kids do. Like give me a break, you're just exaggerating or bragging. I'd much rather hear the honest situations that make you want to pull your hair out so I know I'm not alone. Your social media highlight reel doesn't much impress me. Tell it like it is. Don't sugarcoat things and we'll all be better off for it. Anyway, misery loves company. So, there's that too. But just indulge me a few minutes on her desirable traits.

At the top of that list is the fact she is a solid sleeper. She slept through the night for the first time at six weeks. We, like many first-time parents, started our post-hospital newborn life with her in our room with us. Bliss in our hearts and delirium in our brains. We thought this would be great. Convenient, easier, etc. We had her next to my side of the bed as I would be the one getting up to breastfeed her and that side of the room had the most space. After only a few days, we quickly found out that she was getting up more often than we thought she should be (not that we really knew jack squat at this point but still).

After reading more books, we realized that having your baby sleep in the kitchen, as they say, can cause them to get up more often. If you're like us and have never heard of this phenomenon, let me explain. Think of your favorite food or in the case of a baby, the only food you've ever had. Think about trying to sleep right next to the smell of said food. Probably would be waking you up in the middle of the night with cravings yourself, huh? Makes sense. That's like a lot of things with kids. It makes sense after someone explains it yet when you're a newbie to it all, it doesn't dawn on you. So then only after a few days or so, we decided to go ahead and put her in her nursery.

Fast forward a little over a month and I wake up suddenly. Panicked, I reached for my clock, i.e., my phone, and see that it's 6 a.m. I push Jeff awake and say that Pfeiffer is asleep. Of course, since he, too, is asleep, he doesn't realize what I'm saying. I explain and say that she hasn't woken up. At all. All night. We dart out of bed and into her room to make sure she's still breathing and sure enough, she's simply sleeping soundly. From that night on, she slept through the night. Now, we did end up following some parenting books for schedules and sleep training but it all started there. Hallelujah! Praise the Lord! Insert happy dance here.

While the lack of sleep was one of my biggest concerns with having kids, I, of course, had a plethora of concerns. Will they be happy? Will they be healthy? Will they be smart? Will something Jeff and I do or don't do eff them up physically, emotionally, spiritually for the rest of their life and should we start saving for their therapy sessions now? Will they make friends at school? Will they like us? Will they have an absurd obsession with clowns or tarantulas? How can we be supportive without being helicopter parents? At what age should they get a cell phone? Will they want to get face tattoos? Will they want to live in our house forever and never want to leave? And the list of questions, comments, and concerns get darker and deeper and could go on and on.

Back to sleep or lack thereof. I do not do well when I don't get enough sleep. Ask my husband. What many could hack on six to seven hours of sleep, I need at a minimum of eight. I just can't survive. Okay, that's obviously an exaggeration, but I am on Struggle Street without enough rest. I've always been this way. Let's hope the gamble of having another kid won't totally mess this up for me. Eek.

Let's talk about something for a second. Why are people often quick to point out your kid's flaws as parenting issues or deficits but slow to compliment you or give kudos to you if your kid is great? It's like the bad things are your fault but the good things have nothing to do with you. You're accountable for the bad but not responsible for the good. It's total BS. Jerks.

Before I start to ramble too much to you, back to Pfeiffer. Another wonderful thing about this little chickadee is that she eats great. I bought into the whole idea that the better I ate when I was pregnant, the better eater she would be and also the idea of being strategic about what foods to introduce when. We did veggies first, nothing too sweet, no sugar for a while, etc. Oh, and staying away from artificial colors and flavorings (those things freak me the eff out with all they've been proven to be linked to). And dammit, it has worked. And if it ain't broke, no need to fix it.

As I mentioned, I eat a mostly plant-based diet, or a vixen as my uncle would label it, and she follows my eating patterns. I dropped meat in 5th grade after seeing an animal cruelty video. It shook me to the core and I was physically unable to consume meat afterward. Thus, I clearly have no idea how to even begin to cook meat nor do I care to learn (nor do I need to learn). I don't pretend to be a Michelin star chef but I cook the meals for our family and no one leaves hungry.

One thing both Jeff and I were big on was the idea that we would eat meals together and that there would be no special children's menu. Our kids will eat what we eat. They don't have to like everything but they will try everything. I will not be a short cook catering to their every food whim.

Pfeiffer, behind only my Grandma Pat, is the slowest eater I know, which is a good trait but sometimes it's like watching paint dry. Jeff and I need to have some of that rub off on us because we usually practically inhale our food. Watching her eat reminds me of a commercial I saw where a group of people are playing Pictionary with a sloth and it's almost painful for them as the sloth clearly is the slowest player to ever have played the game.

Watching kids do a variety of things is often like that commercial. We are attempting to foster independence and encourage her to try new things but sometimes we both are silently screaming inside and want to jump in and do it for her.

One morning, I was letting her, with a dull knife (one used to slice a cheese ball or something of the sort), try her hand at cutting her own toast into triangles or squares or whatever she wanted. She insisted on doing it herself, without letting me guide the knife or help provide the adequate amount of pressure needed to actually break through the bread. I eventually had to walk away and pour some more coffee because there was only so much verbal cheerleading I could do. We were running late for school, and to be honest, her techniques and the amount of time it was taking was giving me anxiety.

Besides my eating patterns, she has also picked up my knack for being slightly obsessive compulsive about having things tidy and clean. She has a little toy cleaning set with a broom, dustpan, duster, and mop and uses it on the regular. She also likes to wipe down our kitchen table and countertops. However, she does make a damn mess when she eats. Obviously, I know this is typical for a toddler but she does it on purpose, taking her food off her plate and placing it onto the table, which is surprising, because as I mentioned, she likes things to be clean. Kids are strange.

She also likes to use our small, handheld vacuum when she needs to clean a bigger mess than her broom can handle. Next, we need to get her a real vacuum so she can actually get to work. She also likes to sweep outside. Listen, we allow it. We encourage it. Please don't judge us. Start 'em young, raise 'em right, right?

Here's another scenario that falls into the start 'em young, raise 'em right category. We aren't big on screen time for Pfeiffer and are trying to be really intentional about it. But because Jeff is a sports addict (he would literally watch professional bowling if that was the only sport being broadcasted) and I want to watch the Seminoles, she does get to watch some sports. For the most part it's football or basketball games or golf tournaments (don't get me started on her love for Tiger Woods). The sports often become background noise to her until she hears us cheer or she hears a song on a commercial and then it sparks her interest again. During football games she would always point to the television, no matter who is playing, and say, "Seminoles!" If it's Sunday we'd then have to explain to her that the Seminoles play on Saturdays and the Saints (our favorite professional team) play on Sundays.

It's important to teach your children this type of useless information. We occasionally try to wash it down with having her say the days of the week in English and Spanish to make it a sufficient teaching moment.

The fact that she has been able to adequately do the Seminole chant and tomahawk chop since she could talk or move her arm, I suppose is a form of brainwashing our child. Trying to make her (and of course eventually our second child too) subconsciously, or actually, consciously, like the Seminoles and want to attend Florida State University so that in many years we can still be reliving our college years. Since she'd be there it would somehow be acceptable. Whether it's brainwashing or another case of starting 'em young and raising 'em right, we'll continue to encourage it. Pfeiffer is now very much looking forward to attending her first basketball game and continues to ask almost daily if she and her daddy can go to a game. Soon, baby girl, soon.

So now to tell the crappy things and real-life shitty stuff she does. Things that get under our skin or piss us off or are flat out annoying.

These are usually the funniest things anyway, well at least after you have time to digest the crappiness of whatever it is that's happened. She has begun this awful habit of spitting like a freakin' camel. Okay, well it's not that extreme or aggressive considering it usually ends up on her chin or her shirt but it's the best animal I could think of to compare this nasty behavior to.

I've heard of infants and toddlers biting but haven't heard of many spitting stories. Which would you rather have a biter or a spitter? Ah, the fun games you play with yourself and others when you have kids. We are currently trying to break this habit. Sometimes it's best to tell her no and send her booty straight to timeout (my husband's go-to move). Other times it's best to ignore and not react and see if it passes. I'm hoping this is just a phase. It's just a phase, right?! Tell me it's just a phase. Jeff can't stand it. He has zero tolerance for it. I wonder if he has a traumatic toddler spitting story submerged in his subconscious or maybe it's just because he's been in healthcare for so long and realizes how gross and germ-filled her saliva is.

I don't have a traumatic spitting story from my childhood but I do have a salvia story that still haunts me. The story traces back to first grade. First grade was a great time in my life. Learning all sorts of new and exciting things. I had a great teacher. Life was good. Except for one little boy in my class. When I was in first grade, and for much of my entire life actually, I had long hair. One day I had my hair in a braid and our class was lining up to go outside. I felt a slight tug on my hair and I turned around to catch this kid, Isaac, chewing on my hair! Chewing or sucking or I don't really even know what to call it. I'm not sure if maybe it smelled good and therefore, he thought it would taste good or what his motivation was but Isaac couldn't resist. I'm not sure what ole Isaac is up to these days but let's hope he didn't go off the deep end and that that was his serial killer sign. It is funny the random things you remember that truly have no significance yet, for whatever reason, stick in your head for decades. Kids are filthy creatures.

PMack, like I assume many toddlers, is a master manipulator, I mean negotiator. We try to have a balance of when to give a little bit and when to tighten up with whatever it is. I read a while back that there is a large disparity between the number of times a child hears the word no compared to the word yes. While we are definitely not going to tell her yes every time she asks for something or wants to do something, it has made me mindful and question when I do say the word no. Is it that big of a deal or does it really not matter? Five more minutes in the bath? Yes, sure, go ahead girl, splash on. Playing with knives? No, I don't think so. We have begun using a timer for bedtime and when it alerts us, she always asks, "Means it's bedtime?" We will affirm that it is indeed bedtime and she gets it. She doesn't question it. However, when we, for whatever reason, don't use the timer and just tell her three or five more minutes and then tell her it's bedtime, she wants to bargain. "How about two more minutes?" Girl, you don't even fully understand what one minute is. You can't count up to 60 and you don't know what seconds are compared to minutes yet. I suppose it's easier sometimes for kids to fall in line with someone or something other than their parents, like an inanimate object or Amazon Alexa. That's why they're sometimes angels for a babysitter and demon children for their parents. They feel the need to act right with more of a stranger whereas they feel more comfortable with their parents and therefore, push their boundaries. Fun stuff. Oh, the joys of parenthood.

You do have to watch it though with these little rug rats. For one, give an inch and they take a mile. And two, habits are formed very quickly. This was something I was uber concerned with, or maybe mindful is a better word, from her birth: habits. If we do blank now, she'll always expect or want blank. For example, if you always read one book before bed and then you give and allow them two or three, they will then always want more than one. At least that's the case with her.

Now, back to things being a big deal or not. Extra books are not a huge deal but sometimes you have to weigh the premise of it. Will giving my child this extra book influence her to be a sweet babe and go right to bed willingly afterwards or will she then become an expert negotiator where she can never be satisfied by anything and then all of a sudden is wearing the pants in the relationship? Unfortunately, there's no parenting manual so you just have to guess and pray to God you guessed correctly. Lots of time spent in prayer after having kids that's for sure.

Back to repetition. Habits. Schedules. Kids love it. They love knowing what to expect. It makes them feel comfortable and my guess is, more in control of what can be a scary, unknown world for them. I'm all for a schedule and helping them feel safe and secure, but with that comes drawbacks. What am I referring to you may ask?

Well, this is why they can read books until the pages fall out and it's torn to shreds. This is also why they can hear songs like "Baby Shark" by Pinkfong a trillion times and never get sick of it. That song, by the way, is the most viewed YouTube video ever, which, at the time of writing this book, is over seven billion times. The song has made the Korean family who own Pinkfong millionaires. If I never heard that song again it would be too soon. Luckily, it is no longer a top hit in our house.

A current favorite song of Pfeiffer's is "Let It Go" from the movie *Frozen*. Not quite as annoying as "Baby Shark" but also not ever going to be a chosen tune of mine. Another favorite of hers is what she calls church music. Church music is now a genre for her but when she initially started saying this, we were very confused. She didn't want to merely hear any of the musical selection from church. No. We finally discovered she was referring to one song, "Way Maker", specifically sung by Michael W. Smith and Vanessa Campagna, although she will settle for another version if she must.

It's interesting how you can watch your children change and evolve from saying and doing the things you do and liking the things you like, to beginning to have their own personalities and interests and unique behaviors. Every now and then as a parent you get this glimmer of hope and you smile and think that maybe you are doing something right and it helps you keep chugging along. Since we are a faith-based family, seeing her sing and dance to church music is one of these moments. Then your child acts a fool in public over some BS and you're back to the mind eff that is parenthood.

She can now adequately use the aforementioned Amazon Alexa and therefore can play whatever song she'd like. Well, that is when she knows the name of the song or at least when Alexa can understand her, which both PMack and Alexa are getting good at. When she was about two, she was trying to request a song. She kept telling me and Alexa that she wanted to hear "Somebody Who Knows You" or "Somebody Who Loves You". I didn't know these song titles and Alexa would try her best and play a random song but Pfeiffer would have a fit because it wasn't the song she wanted. But finally, after her persistently asking and me continuing to try to decode what she was wanting, I realized she wanted to hear "I Wanna Dance with Somebody" by Whitney Houston. This quickly became her most requested song. Apparently, they play this song at her school. I've never envisioned this song as a song for kiddos but it does make sense. It's an upbeat song. It's fun. I've danced many a time to this song at parties and weddings (and, as we've already covered, in dive bars singing karaoke). But one drawback to this song is that it's over five minutes long. It's not over quickly like "Baby Shark". For this song you have to just face the music and attempt to jam out and enjoy it. Over and over again. But we want her to listen to non-kid music so I'll take 20 minutes of Whitney on repeat as the tradeoff.

Taking after her father, she can freestyle songs like the best of them. She will randomly make up lyrics to songs and they will rhyme. She started doing this around her second birthday, which, to me, seems very impressive. I can barely put full sentences together some days and yet my toddler can string like-sounding words together in a clever and creative way? Okay, that's cool, right? Now her vocabulary is not extremely vast at the moment so sometimes her rhyming words consist of those such as poop or puppy, but still, she's a bright little person. One of her best rhymes to date was "If that mockingbird don't shine, momma's gonna buy you a glass of wine". She could barely get that lyric out without smiling from ear to ear. Jeff and I lost it with laughter. She was extremely proud of herself. As were we. It also made us evaluate our occasional wino tendencies.

To revert to annoying things she does and to continue on the topic of poop, she has been saying there's poop everywhere. She has a strange fascination with poop. I say that it's strange but maybe this is normal for kids? I'm not sure. Let me be clear that when she points to something and exclaims that it is poop, there is not, in fact, poop right there. Except when she's following our dog out in the yard and she uses the bathroom. And by she, I am actually referring to both our Chesapeake Bay Retriever, Hartley, as well as Pfeiffer, who has now taken a poop out in our backyard. I'm sure our neighborhood's homeowner association would very much disapprove of this. I'll just be thankful it didn't happen in the front yard at the risk of us getting fined. Maybe she simply likes talking about poop because she is somewhat newly potty trained? Or again, maybe this is all part of what is normal but seems bizarre to those who are first-time parents. I don't want poop to be the center of every conversation. It drives me crazy but I've also realized that sometimes the things you harp on the most or give the most attention to, are the things kids (and sometimes husbands) want to do the most so I try to not let the silliness of the poop situation drive me too bonkers.

Along with her freestyling of songs, she also will create her own little mashups to songs she knows. The other day she combined "Itsy Bitsy Spider" with "Baa, Baa Black Sheep". It was a catchy little tune.

Another thing she's received from her father is what is turning out to look like some pretty solid athletic abilities. I enjoy working out and am very much into fitness. I even enjoy watching sports. Over the years, I even played sports growing up but they were never my main passion. As I mentioned, I was a ballet dancer for 15 years. That was my thing. Loved it then and I still do. We will see if PMack is interested in that as well. She definitely already has rhythm and loves to boogie.

But she has shown a strong interest in golf. She has already dabbled with many golf clubs and hit plenty of balls. Jeff always claims that women's golf scholarships are the most unclaimed scholarships for college athletics and with his golf obsession I think he would absolutely love it if she truly takes a liking to and has strong skills in this sport. Again, we shall see.

For the most part, there isn't a lot that I don't enjoy doing with Pfeiffer. This, of course, is when she isn't whining or pretending to hit me or acting like a twat. I mean acting not like the little lady she is.

When I'm talking about the things I enjoy doing, I mostly mean this to include the things in her world. Things like playing and coloring and exploring and such. To be honest, I absolutely would rather not grocery shop with her or run most of my errands with her. Sort of amusing because Jeff loves taking her to run errands, I suppose then he doesn't have to go alone and we know he prefers that. But overall, she's just a cool chic. She's fun and she really cracks me up. She's got a good energy about her. Before you roll your eyes or dry-heave, I am not stating this to say that parenthood is the best thing ever and thinking that I am some type of supermom because I just adore my daughter and everything about her. I don't think that or feel that. In fact, I truly struggled when I was able to stay at home with my daughter. This could have either been my bout with severe postpartum depression or maybe I enjoy her more now that I am not staying home with her. Or maybe it's a combination of both. I am not the Pinterest mom or the highlight reel mom but I will say that I have tried my damndest to enjoy each stage in her life thus far. I have found that I loved the infant stage and having practically no responsibilities but learning how to keep a newborn alive and staring at her for the majority of the day. As she gets older and more independent, I am enjoying hanging out with her and find myself fascinated by her little personality and big brain and sense of humor.

While some of you are wanting to give me a glaring look and I probably would be too, let me say that this is not the case 24 hours a day, seven days per week. Not by any means. Not anywhere close. There are times when I spaz out on her more than I like. When I lose my patience or my temper and cry at the fact I did, then sometimes laugh at the fact I did shed tears and think, once again, about the mind eff this whole parenting thing is.

There are days when she spends plenty of time in timeout. But overall, I enjoy her and I would wish that upon everyone I know who has kids. This may also be in part because she really likes me. "Mommy's a best friend," she will say, although she says her dad is too and I'm good with that. It's nice to feel wanted and on the top of someone's cool list, even if that person is a toddler. She's also way more fun than I expected or knew any kid could be. She's funny and clever and constantly keeps me laughing with the shit she says and the random things she does.

"Mommy, why are your teeth so big?" "Mommy, why do you use so much toilet paper?" "Mommy, want to see my down dog and summersault?" And let me also say that I understand she very well may become a little shit sooner rather than later. I am not the parent who is naïve and thinks that her child is the best and will always be the best and will never upset or disappoint or be a nuisance or anything like that. I am optimistic about how she will turn out, but I am a realist when understanding the hell we may have to go through, especially when thinking about what Jeff and I dished out to our parents and the trouble we sometimes put them through.

Back to less than desirable traits of Pfeiffer's. This little girl is fairly conceited or maybe a nicer way to express this is that she is fixated on herself. She always wants to look at pictures of herself. I'm not sure if all kids are like that but I am sure that she did not acquire that attribute from me. I don't pretend to be photogenic so you won't catch me casually wanting to review pictures of myself. She always wants to catch a glimpse of herself in the mirror or in a window's reflection. During dinner time she will look back towards the window that looks out to our back porch and will simply stare at herself off and on while she eats her meal. I'm glad it's not a window that my neighbors could see. They'd probably be wondering why she was constantly staring at them or their house. Yet another thing she didn't get from me. If I'm at a restaurant with mirrors, I don't want to be anywhere close to them. I don't need a constant visual of myself chomping down. I suppose they would be quite nice to have on a first date though; make sure there's no spinach in your teeth, check to see that your hair remains on point, etc.

It drives me absolutely bonkers when she won't allow us to style her hair. Let me explain because I don't want you assuming I'm the mom who must have her child's hair exactly perfect with a gigantic bow on top. I think that's cute and respect the mommas who do this, but no, that's not me. Pfeiffer's hair is getting very long and it's constantly in her face. So, with her often unwillingness to let us pull it back and her inability to put it behind her ears, it's almost always over at least part of one of her eyes. HOW CAN ANYONE STAND THAT?! My anxiety also flairs up a bit with that. That would absolutely drive me insane and I think anyone who has ever had hair long enough for this to be a concern would also agree. It's sort of interesting she won't let us do more with her hair, too, because she has this idea that hair ties help make people pretty so, I would think she would be all about them.

Allow me to clarify this a bit more. One day we asked Pfeiffer how she got to be so pretty and she responded, "Hair ties." I mean, they absolutely do help with our appearance, I'll give you that, girlfriend. But no, she knew that we'd often tell her how great she looked after we were done getting her dressed and doing her hair (the times she actually lets us style it) and therefore, she knew exactly how to answer that question. She plays to her audience. It's funny to ask kids random questions to get their off-the-wall or spot-on accurate answers. To look on the bright side, I guess even though she's vain, we should be happy she isn't overly concerned yet with the idea of looking pretty. Although, if she was, she'd at least let us use some hair ties (since they make you pretty) and she'd be able to see a bit better. Can't win 'em all.

So, this next statement is two-fold because while it happens because Pfeiffer is not being good, it also happens to be very humorous. Sometimes when she's testing her limits we'll ask if she's making smart choices or give her the look. Now whether you're a parent or not, you know the look. Everyone knows this look. This is the one your mom would shoot over to you if you were giggling in church with your friends or acting up in the grocery store in front of people. It's a look that seems to say, "This is a warning but if you continue what you're doing, you're going to be in trouble." When she admits to not listening or being a sweet girl, she'll often say, "I need to go to timeout". She'll put herself in her timeout spot and then come back after about 30 seconds and tell us she's ready to listen now. Sometimes when we put her in timeout she'll come out after only a few seconds and once again say she's ready to listen. Now girlfriend, you can come out of the timeout you voluntarily place yourself into when you find the time is right but it doesn't work that way when your mommy or daddy puts you there. At that point, you have done the crime and you have got to serve your time, which, for those of you wondering, is only about two minutes (one minute for each year she's been alive).

We've had positive success with timeout. We will usually give her a few chances, depending on what she's doing and whether or not we have a zero-tolerance policy for that specific behavior, and then if she doesn't shape up, she'll go into her little spot on the wall designated for timeout. There, we will reiterate to her what she's done to be serving her time and then during her alone time she either screams or cries or just sits there quietly (or a combination of all three) and then after the time is over, we will come ask her if she's ready to listen and not do whatever it was that got her in trouble. We'll offer her a hug, which she always accepts, and then more times than not she comes back with a better attitude. Sometimes we all just need our own timeout. We just need a moment to ourselves. Whether it's time away from others or simply to remove yourself from a situation, we can often return with a fresh perspective and a better, happier attitude. Instead of getting overworked up and overwhelmed and frustrated, take a moment to pause, step away, simply breathe or be alone. Try it sometime.

We've all either personally been there or we've overheard other parents applauding their child for doing what we as adults would perceive as a miniscule task. "Great job climbing into the car little Timmy." "Way to go not peeing in your pants while we were in that store and asking me when you needed to go to the bathroom sweet Pfeiffer." Honestly, the compliments I have given to Pfeiffer since she's been born, I would like to have given to me. I do have to give her some kudos though because as of late, when Jeff and I finish our dinner, she'll point it out and congratulate us on doing such a good job. This is nice, but probably a better form of praise when it comes to eating would be for her to applaud if I don't go back for a second helping. But in all seriousness, when do people stop congratulating you for doing simple things? When do we stop feeling good about ourselves for accomplishing basic things? I guess once you become an adult these things are just expected, which I understand but sometimes it's beyond nice and even motivating to hear "Attagirl!" "Good job!" "You're doing great at life!" Adulting can be hard some days and if more people simply told us that we did a great job getting dressed and that we looked nice, we'd probably be a happier and more confident society. And the same goes with stickers. I want stickers for adulting. They're a tangible, constant reminder of the compliment someone gave you. "Great job on getting a physical." "Congrats on not buying Twinkies at the grocery store."

Having kids makes me relive my childhood in my head. Recently, now that my daughter can ask for more and is having her own interests, I'm excited to see what will be popular toys in our house. Well, I'm equally excited as I am dreading it. I don't want a bunch of annoying things in our house so we will work to combat that. She loves some of my old Beanie Babies. Yes, I still held onto some of them. This is a solid win considering that since I never sold them and made millions, they might as well get used and, as an added perk, they don't make noise. Remember Furby? Somewhat cute, somewhat slightly demonic. They're trying to make a comeback but I'm not sure it'll catch on. Oh, what will the new trends be that we will look back at in 20 years and laugh at? I may say those LOL Dolls but I'm not sure I'll ever smile thinking of those. Those are an awful gift. Let's get our children a toy with a billion little pieces for you to step on and have strung throughout your home, never to be found again after unpackaging. No. No, thank you. Troll dolls, since the 1960s, have gone through their ups and downs in popularity and were a hit when I was a kid. It's too bad my mom had this notion they were sort of demonic so she never let us have any.

To this day, one of the funniest Halloween costumes I've ever seen is when a guy friend of mine dressed up as a Troll while we were in high school simply by dying his hair green and gelling it up high and wearing shorts with nothing on his top half except for a giant jewel glued where his belly button was. Simple yet so, so good. The trolls that are popular now I think my mom would approve of. They're more glitter and love than anything evil, although I'm not sure her original suspicions were even warranted. Furbies on the other hand, those very well may have been possessed by something unholy.

I miss Tamogotchi. Our electronics were so much simpler back then. Kids these days don't know how advanced they have it. Yes, I did just say, "Kids these days," as if I'm 95 years old and I'm shaking my fist in the air. We were happy with a two-inch screen and a black and white imaginary pet. Although, our Nintendo Game Boy, color-version, was pretty advanced, right? I think they would enjoy that nowadays. One thing I don't really want to get my daughter are those baby dolls that act like real infants. Why do kids have an obsession with kids who are tinier than they are? And why would I want to add another crying child who also wets herself and needs to eat to my family? I'm going to fight that one as long as I can. I think I still have my Doodle Bear with all my piss-poor handwriting and drawings. What will be next? Oh, the suspense. And also, a friendly little PSA for you, if you remember the toys I just mentioned, you want to make sure that you're now following a daily night cream regimen.

After having kids, I find that I always instinctively, and unaware, choose a spot to sit on the floor. I was at my in-laws' house recently and just sat down on their carpet next to the children and the toys. Pfeiffer had her cousins there to play with. I really had no reason to sit on the floor other than just the habitualness of it all. I'd fit in well in Asian countries with their practices of floor culture. It's funny the routine and habits you come into when you have kids. The unconscious things you do on a day-to-day basis. Some of which may or may not include, always carrying extra food with you and some type of sanitary wipes and of course a toy, swearing off places that don't have changing tables in their restrooms, constantly scoping out restaurants that offer free or discounted kid's meals and the list could go on.

"Have kids," they said. "It'll be fun," they said. In all seriousness, having PMack and now preparing for baby number two, has been some of the highlights of my life. Kids make everything harder but, in my opinion, make everything better. I believe it is true what they say about having children: they make a good marriage, better, and a bad marriage, worse. So just a little advice to not have a baby in hopes of saving your marriage. Odds are it won't work the way you want it to.

I sometimes long for the simplicity of life without kids but then I remember I can have the joy of having kids while also having the pleasure of being an irresponsible kid at heart reliving any immature whim I want whenever I'd like thanks to the option of being able to utilize grandparents who live only a couple of hours away. Score. Thank the Lord for them and for paid babysitters. Taking a break and being simply you the person, not the mom, caregiver, meal-maker, etc., is a vital part of being a parent, at least for me.

And it's vital for my marriage. We have to be able to reconnect with one another during a time that doesn't include dinner with a toddler making a mess and constantly telling us to look at her face or saying "Excuse me." I need to be able to kick my kid off my leg (figuratively of course) and recharge. Bye Felicia. Quality time is one of love languages in case you haven't picked up on that. And not even only that, just having a break is important. Don't do anything. Just relax. That's also equally important. It's healthy to not adult on occasion. Also, if you're ever super annoyed with your kids and want a total brain numb, check out #whymykidiscrying on social media as well as the Kids Getting Hurt Instagram account. It'll make you feel less alone and also just make you pee your pants in the ridiculousness and hysterics that is, having kids.

People have asked us if there are things we will do differently with our next baby. Any lessons we've learned the hard way and want to not repeat. I'm sure there are but it's incredible how quickly you black things out. It is said that this is a habit of many people and a reason why people continue to have children (this and maybe because they like doing the act of what leads to having kids, if you catch my drift). People forget about the crappy things and let the good overshadow everything else.

Also, I learned quickly, before even having kids, to never say that I would or wouldn't do something when having kids. I never wanted my words to come back and bite me in the booty and I never wanted to offend anyone with my opinions regarding children. I would suggest telling all the people you know to try to do the same. But to answer the question of what we will do when we have baby number two: we will survive. We will be in full-blown survival mode with a toddler and a newborn on our hands. And I'm sure we will utilize the previously mentioned grandparents a lot more often. May the odds be ever in our favor.

LESSONS LEARNED:

- If you have multiple kids, you won't have to share your love, your heart simply grows.
- Enjoy things like children do. It always seems to be the little things that children appreciate and we should learn to follow suit. We should be in awe of the world. Aim to look at it with new eyes and a fresh perspective. And never lose that sense of wonder.
- Recognize people for simple things. Sometimes just telling them that they are doing great at life (or insert another specific sentiment) is all it takes to turn their week around.
- Give yourself a timeout when you need one.
- You never know what random traits you'll pass onto your children or that others will pick up on and gain from you; try to make it good.

FINAL THOUGHTS

Thank you for reading. I hope you've enjoyed a look inside a handful of my silly family members. And I hope it's given you even just a little bit of insight to look at your family in ways that you may not have before. Also, keep in mind that the term "family" doesn't simply include the family you're born into or born with. They aren't only the biological people in your life; they're also the people you choose to be in your life. The friends who turn into family. The people who you place in your life by choice or come along by chance. What can they teach you? What lessons can you learn because of them or in spite of them?

Or, just as importantly, I hope it's made you chuckle.

In some way, shape, or form, we all can be a freakin' mess in need of help and a hardy laugh. Take the best of people and model their behavior. Take their worst and learn from it. Make it humorous. Make it enjoyable. Make it loveable.

And remember: it'll be okay.

ACKNOWLEDGMENTS

I want to first acknowledge you, the reader. Thank you, again, for reading this book. I am extremely grateful for you. Next, a special thank you to the family members in the book for allowing me to chat about you. I also want to thank my other family and my friends who, from the start, have been supportive of this passion project of mine. Furthermore, a big thanks to the various people I reached out to along the way for random advice, feedback, and brainstorming sessions (you know who you are and I appreciate you). Last but certainly not least, a huge thank you to my editor, Bob Howard. You've helped me grow as a writer and I am honored and blessed to be able to gain from your expertise.

ABOUT THE AUTHOR

Erika Bell is a lifelong writer and small business owner. Her first published book was the children's story *The Little Albino Dino and His Big Friend Rhino*. As a lover of all things self-help and humor, Erika, who with her large extended family knows about the idiosyncrasies of family members, decided to combine all of these themes to write her second book, *Family, Funnies, and Other F Words*. Whether fiction or nonfiction, for children or adults, her books all hold commonalities and weave together humor, a jovial nature, and an appreciation for others.

Erika holds a master's degree from Florida State University and currently lives in Tallahassee, Florida with her hubby, two kids, and pup. She has a deep love for traveling, spending time with family, boating, and peanut butter. She enjoys a difficult puzzle, a good glass of champagne, and the frequent F-word.

Erika looks forward to sharing her writing for years to come. Find out more, connect, and stay up-to-date on what's next at erikareidbell.com and @erikareidbell on social media.